DOWN SOUTH + EAST

DOWN SOUTH + EAST

A CHINESE AMERICAN COOKBOOK

Ron Hsu WITH Hugh Amano

PHOTOGRAPHS BY Rinne Allen

FOREWORD BY Eric Ripert

ABRAMS, NEW YORK

For my late mother, Betty, who instilled in me a foundation of values that helped me get to where I am today;

Jackie, my beautiful wife, who enabled me to chase my dreams and is a continued source of inspiration;

and my daughter, Calliope, who keeps me grounded every day and enriches my life to the fullest.

Contents

Foreword

BY CHEF ERIC RIPERT

Great chefs are shaped not just by mastering cookery technique, but by the stories they carry, the places they have called home, and the flavors that have left a mark on them. This no doubt applies to the author of this book, Chef Ron Hsu. Ron worked with us for many years in the kitchen at Le Bernardin. I am very grateful for the time he worked for us at the restaurant—he became an integral part of our team and worked his way up from line cook to sous chef, and eventually to head of creativity. He was and is a team player and a great cook. Nothing makes me happier than seeing former chefs or employees of Le Bernardin go on to pursue their dreams and succeed. I expected nothing less from Ron, who has made a name for himself as a successful restaurateur.

In this book, Ron pays homage to the cooking of the people and places that had an influence on him, especially that of his mother. He is a Chinese American who grew up in the American South. This unique combination is what makes Ron's food distinctively his. I would say this concept applies to most chefs—the food we were exposed to at an early age usually has a significant effect on the chefs we become. Ron would often come to me during creative development for the menu concerned his dishes leaned heavily Asian. I always told him that was more than OK and to listen to his inner chef. His life experiences have paved the way to create his unique cooking style. It is ultimately each of our life differences that make our cooking styles different from the cook next to us on the line.

One might think it would be counterintuitive to mix the flavors of Asian countries with those of the American South, but Ron teaches us in this book that food can transcend cultural barriers. We see many examples of this with his recipes such as Kimchi and Okra Stew, Collard Green Fried Rice, or Barbecue Brisket and Rice Cake Stir Fry, to name a few. To our surprise, these unexpected pairings turn out to be harmonious and delicious. Consider this book a reframing of the expected labels of food as "Asian" or "Southern" and an inspiration—there are no limitations to what can define a certain cuisine and make it great. Throughout the eight chapters, you will find an abundance of recipes as creative and comforting as these, spanning across different ingredients, including vegetables, beef, rice, noodles, and more. His recipes will take you on a journey through Ron's mind and palate as chef. In this book, we see Ron's vast knowledge, his style of food, and his creativity. These recipes he has shared are a surprise and delight, and I know you will enjoy reading and cooking them as much as I have.

Introduction

You hold in your hands a book that serves as a guide to making delicious, innovative Asian-influenced dishes via the rich larder of the American South, soulful dishes relevant to today's increasingly global kitchens. Consider this book a reframing of what can be considered Southern food, and documentation of how local produce and tradition can coexist with global history and culture in one particular place—as interpreted by one particular cook.

Who am I, you ask? I'm Ron Hsu. I'm Chinese. I'm American. A son of the South and of a legendary matriarch of a Chinese restaurant empire in Georgia. But much has happened since my mother immigrated to this country from Malaysia, from the early days I spent in her restaurants growing up in a world galaxies apart from my peers, to my time at one of the best restaurants in the world, Le Bernardin, to opening my own restaurants to critical acclaim. And perhaps closest to my heart, becoming a father to a daughter whose favorite foods include both dim sum and mac and cheese, both readily available in Atlanta, the Southern city we call home.

My story originates in Georgia, a center of social change, a key electoral state, a state with strong food traditions. And as a chef, I'm creating new traditions. I'll share with you what I love to do every day of my life, in the place I want to do it, and with the people and ingredients I want to be doing it with. The recipes in the pages to follow are very personal to me; they are influenced by the food I grew up eating, the cultures surrounding me throughout my life, and my own experience as a chef.

A lot of children of immigrants are now putting their generation's stamp on the food of their homeland, creating new branches of cuisine all over the country. So, my story is very much an American one, and I hope my style of cooking speaks to this current moment, the ever-evolving American palate, and what we are excited to eat. Just as you can now find hoisin sauce, miso paste, or sriracha in the local Piggly Wiggly that once carried no ingredient more exotic than soy sauce, I want this cookbook to build on our growing exposure to different cultures, expanding on existing traditions, opening new possibilities.

I also hope that the harmony found on a plate between once worlds-apart ingredients and techniques can inspire as a vehicle to bring people together. I believe that even simple exposure to seemingly "exotic" ingredients can help encourage connections between people who look different and come from different backgrounds.

And in a much more practical sense, familiarity with a range of ingredients and techniques can be a quick path to flavor—an easy way to make your daily cooking more exciting and delicious.

Through the eight chapters in this book organized by type of ingredient—vegetables, beef, rice, noodles, and

more—you'll find recipes suited to your interests, while also being introduced to new flavors and techniques I've developed for your kitchen. Even though I am a chef and restaurateur, these are recipes that I intentionally developed for the home cook. This is what I like to cook at home and think you will as well, while celebrating ingredients native to the American South and beyond.

The South is full of rich farmlands and waterways, but it's not just the agricultural opulence that has influenced me; my hometown's cultural richness allows me to expand my perspective on food, cooking, and hospitality every day. Living here means I know the best kind of cornbread—made with pork cracklings—can be even better with deeply flavored lap cheong (Chinese sausage). I can easily switch from collards, the traditional Southern hearty green, to more delicate watercress for deliciously light braised greens with a gingery pot likker. Southern sorghum syrup serves as a fantastic glaze for sablefish for my take on Nobu's iconic miso black cod or, with a bit of bourbon, for pork ribs lacquered in the style of char siu. Asian persimmons are prevalent in the American South in desserts like persimmon pudding and pie; peanuts associated with Georgia are commonly marinated and served as a snack in Chinese cooking. Throughout my life, I have been lucky to experience the great beauty of being exposed to different cultures, and it has forever enriched my cooking.

And this is why I'm telling the story of my childhood, which put the spirit of transcending cultural barriers into my DNA, and my adult years as a professional chef in this book. I want to inspire you to explore a market you've never been in, to see and taste ingredients you've never heard of. To understand why they are used as they traditionally are, and to think of how you can use them in other, unexpected ways. To think about why soy sauce would enhance a traditional pot roast (page 176), or why seemingly strange bedfellows like caviar and buttermilk would combine to create a deep, salty-sour richness to be sopped up with steamed milk buns (page 231). Or to recognize that crisp, cool summer rolls stuffed with shrimp pulled from the estuaries off the nearby Gulf of Mexico and dipped in Georgia peanut sauce are as American as they are Vietnamese (page 135). To move past tradition and consider a Chinese-style scallion pancake (page 211) as a serious upgrade to a standard blini for caviar topped with crème fraîche.

Fortunately, I live in a place where I can embrace this spirit of exploration every day, a place with no shortage of ingredients, ingredients that supply not only the traditional cuisines of the American South, but the Chinese food I grew up with, the technique-driven French food I learned in school, and the highly refined haute cuisine I produced at Le Bernardin. Atlanta is a place where I can continue growing, absorbing the incredible international representation of the cultures that make up our community. On Buford Highway on our north side, near a school where I learned Chinese many years ago, a rich, varied ethnic presence in the form of restaurants using and stores selling ingredients like rau ram (Vietnamese cilantro), banana blossoms, and homemade gochujang has expanded along with my understanding of them and the people behind them.

When I was a kid, I assumed these markets only served the Chinese community, but they actually supply ingredients and inspiration for cuisines representing the entire world, cuisines both traditional and innovative. I see more than ever the depth of other Asian cultures as I browse steaming pots of Korean and Japanese dumplings not far from the bowls of Vietnamese pho I had as a kid. A strong Eastern European population has opened me up to an expanded world of cheeses, breads, and pickled vegetables. Over to the east of Atlanta, the DeKalb Farmers Market is especially dense with African ingredients like Mauritanian dates and Ethiopian chiles and injera. And this doesn't only exist in Atlanta. Thanks to today's ever-increasing global community and the availability of ingredients through mail order and web-based sources, new and exciting products are widely accessible to cooks the world over. That might seem like an overwhelming number of new elements to explore, but as a start, this book focuses on guiding you through any Chinese or Southern ingredients that could be new to you.

My fascination with food set in when I was very young, perhaps seven or eight years old. Maybe it happened when I was doing my part by chasing chickens around our Georgia backyard into the waiting arms of my grandmother, who would quickly dispatch the birds, plucking and hanging them outside to bleed just as she had done in Malaysia (and just as so many grandmothers have done in the American South) to make one of our favorite dinners, Soy-Braised Chicken (page 186), slowly cooked with ginger, green onions, and star anise. Or perhaps it was at the table, when my sister noticed my unusual laser focus as I assembled different combinations of our meals; I was building the perfect bites out of the meat, the sauce, and the starch, studying how different combinations interacted, relishing the original dish while learning how different flavors and textures worked together to become something greater than the sum of a dish's parts. Or maybe it was when I'd look through *Restaurant Informer*, the free magazine sent to restaurants by the Georgia Restaurant Association, exploring all the different styles of food out there in the world beyond our kitchen, wondering why that food looked so different from ours, dreaming of ways I might be able to make food that looked like that, too. In short, what I can say for certain is that food has always been front and center in my life. The entire core of my being was built around food, built in restaurants that not only fed a whole lot of Americans on the outskirts of Atlanta, but helped many an immigrant gain a foothold in this country. I learned much more than the effect of heat and seasoning on an ingredient; I learned how food can be a common language that connects, and joins, and fills far more than stomachs.

Beyond the kitchen, it wasn't easy growing up as one of the few Asian kids in my hometown, where few people looked like me. As a child, my mother would drive my siblings and me from one side of Atlanta to the other to the international food and shopping mecca along Buford Highway. The main

mission was the weekly Chinese lesson that I now wish I'd paid more attention to, but my siblings and I would also get to see our cousins, and mom got to shop with my aunts, hanging out on the plaza across from the school gossiping and catching up. And we'd get to eat big, fun meals, meals that other people cooked, us kids running around between bites of dim sum, or char siu over rice, or sometimes Vietnamese pho. Plus, this sanctuary along Atlanta's northeast side offered refuge from the embedded, casual racism at school and in our small neighborhood on the outskirts of Atlanta. On Buford Highway, playing with my cousins while my mom and aunts drank tea nearby meant there was none of that to worry about; no one mistook me as Mexican simply because I wasn't Black or White. It was a place of belonging.

Back home, I was fortunate to have a strong base from which to navigate the world as well. My father was a lifelong chef, who trained in Malaysia, and was the main man behind the wok in our restaurants, but beyond his technical skill, it was my mother's approach toward helping others that defined for me the value of reaching a hand out rather than doing the easy thing and turning away when someone needed help. One by one, she brought cooks and dishwashers, servers and business partners—the whole gamut of restaurant workers—into her growing empire of restaurants (and often our home), using food as a way to help family and strangers alike get a start in this country, just as she'd done so many years ago. And there were efforts to take the best of both worlds and combine them culinarily. Cans of cream of mushroom soup would, at times, serve as a braising medium for chicken; even better was her Meatloaf with Shiitake Mushrooms (page 171), far more flavorful than the school lunch version you are probably imagining, richly seasoned with a soy sauce and ketchup glaze. During holidays—when our family hosted a house full of cousins, aunts, uncles, and friends—before breaking out the mahjong set, my mother, Betty, would roast turkey and open canned cranberry sauce (I would be in charge of microwaving the Stove Top stuffing), but then we'd also always have a beautiful steamed fish with long beans and fried noodles. The turkey bones would be turned into stock; the next day the stock would be flavored with goji berries and the Chinese dates known as *jujubes*, ladled over shredded duck (or leftover turkey) and wheat noodles, and topped with a generous handful of sliced green onions before we gathered around the table to slurp it all down.

Meanwhile, I loved being in the kitchen at my mother's restaurants. Born in Malaysia to Chinese parents wed at age twelve in a prearranged marriage, she attended college before coming to this country in the seventies, landing in California before moving the family to Georgia in the eighties, ultimately opening five Chinese restaurants on the outskirts of Atlanta. I grew up in these restaurants, all named Hunan Village followed by a number denoting their order of arrival (skipping four and six, inauspicious in Chinese for their similarity to words meaning "death" and "decline," respectively). My earliest roots as a chef sprouted in these restaurants, especially Hunan Village 1, a previously unsanctioned spot on the school bus route where, due to a special deal my mom brokered with the school district, I would be dropped off each afternoon. Starting at the age of nine, I'd push through the glass doors at the front of the restaurant to immediately hit my homework in the dining room, then I'd head to the back kitchen to peel onions by the fifty-pound bagful. I felt like I was on a pirate ship—and I relished it! I got to hang out with the crew of rough (and sometimes hungover) Chinese, Indonesian, Korean, and Mexican cooks, eating things like sesame chicken wrapped in warm corn tortillas with Chinese broccoli while exploring these other cultures through the cooks' vibrant stories. I became a dishwasher at age twelve, and shortly thereafter moved up to the fry station, cooking up crispy egg rolls, chicken wings, and crab Rangoon, simply loving the kitchen life and becoming obsessed with food. During family trips to the Asian markets, I'd run straight for the shrimp chips or the hanging meats and was fascinated by the variety of fresh noodles. I won't say no to a perfect French croissant, but to this day I crave the doughy, dense, less laminated croissants sold in the bakeries of these markets, like the DeKalb Farmers Market, where my grandmother once worked.

Later, while studying business at the University of Georgia, I realized I was fulfilled by the restaurant work I was doing to put myself through school far more than the classes it was paying for. I thought back to a lesson my Uncle Tony (a great wok cook himself and a regular Swiss Army knife of a handyman) taught me when showing me how to make fried rice at Hunan Village. "You can do anything you want with fried rice! Put whatever you have, whatever you like into it. There's no one single way to make fried rice!" And it hit me: The same thing applied to my life. Here I was in school, following a path—a recipe if you will—climbing a ladder I didn't want to reach the top of, forgetting that I had the same absolute freedom now to do whatever I wanted with my life as I did back when choosing the ingredients for that fried rice. I consulted my mom, certain she was going to make me finish out my degree, and got the opposite reaction. She encouraged me to embrace my passion and chase my dreams, and that's exactly what I did. I left Georgia, and ever the lover of challenges and mixing in with other misfits, enrolled in culinary school in Australia, and that was that. My short hiccup outside of the food world was corrected, sending me on a trajectory that would take me around the world, into one of the best (and toughest) kitchens on earth at Le Bernardin, and finally, to open my own restaurants in my old neck of the woods.

These days, some of the trials of being a chef and restaurant owner echo my early racial identity challenges. Before opening my first restaurant, Lazy Betty, people really wanted to put it and my cooking in a certain box, be it French, Chinese, or fusion. But I felt then (and still believe now) that the food I cook fits in none and all of those categories at the same time, that it transcends the simplicity of cultural labels. And that is what you'll find in this book. We'll cook many types of food together throughout these pages, but you can expect a focus on Chinese techniques and ingredients (with some Korean, Japanese, Thai, and Vietnamese), influenced by my experience coming from the South.

Meanwhile, I'm a father now, so more than ever, it isn't just about me. That realigns and reconfirms a lot of my priorities and perspectives around both the food my

family and I eat and the way I approach the world and those I meet. I see a lot of how my mom raised me coming to the surface, and I see a lot of her in my daughter, too. At seven years old, she's already showing the passion, the kindness, the strength of her grandmother. And she loves food, mauling foie gras pâté from my restaurant made with the finest French technique just as easily as juice from kimchi made with Georgia cabbage poured over steamed rice. And sometimes, just as I would when chasing those chickens years ago, she helps make dinner. She'll tightly grasp my paring knife, slowly mincing spring onions for dumplings, transferring them with tiny, cupped hands to a bowl full of pork, ginger, and cabbage. I'll mix the filling together, and I'll take my station next to my little daughter's kitchen counter perch, my wife on the opposite side. Then, we'll join each other in folding dumplings as she, a little chef like her father and her grandmother, issues commands to her crew. As we place each dumpling on a waiting pan, it slowly but steadily fills like so many times before in my life, and in that moment, three generations of Chinese southerners are connected, bonded by a legacy of food and cooking. Here's hoping that the recipes in this book become traditions for your family, evolving with you and yours as they pass from old hands to new and back again through the generations to come.

紹興料酒
SHAOHSING RICE COOKING WINE
NƯỚC MẮM NHỈ
Việt Hương
THREE CRABS Brand
李錦記
LEE KUM KEE
海鮮醬
HOISIN SAUCE
Tương Ăn Phở
NET WT./CÂN NẶNG 20 oz (1 lb 4 oz)
PANDA BRAND
OYSTER FLAVORED SAUCE
NET WT: 8oz(227g)
FROM THE LAND OF TENNESSEE
ONE QUART 32 FL. OZ.
100% GENUINE SORGHUM
DELICIOUS ON BISCUITS CORN BREAD PANCAKES
Muddy Pond
Sorghum Mill
The GUENTHER Family
미원
味元
SINCE 1956
250 g

Pantry

Ingredients that are instrumental to my cooking are listed below. They might stand out as Southern or Asian ingredients (or ingredients from any number of cuisines, for that matter), but however you categorize them, they are essential to me. Nowadays, these ingredients are pretty accessible, whether in grocery stores, Asian markets (if you are fortunate enough to have one nearby), or online. Note that I'll list a brand name when I have a favorite; otherwise, anything you can find will do.

BUTTERMILK

Tangy buttermilk is a widely used ingredient in the South, not just in baking (Lap Cheong Cornbread, page 120), but in dressings and dips (Crispy Rice Sticks with Sriracha Ranch, page 84) and marinades (Buttermilk Fried Chicken, page 194) as well. I prefer the full-fat version, but if you're having problems with it curdling—which it can do when heated too much or incorporated with too much acid—simply use buttermilk powder instead, found online or in a specialty store.

COLLARD GREENS

Collards are the most iconic Southern vegetable, if you ask me—far too versatile to only be braised with ham hocks (as tasty and essential as that is). I especially love this cousin to cauliflower in stir-fries like the Collard Green Fried Rice (page 73), Stir-Fried Egg Noodles with Collard Greens and Eggs (page 237), and Stir-Fried Beef with Fermented Black Beans and Collard Greens (page 163). Sliced thinly enough, these greens even work raw in a salad a la kale. Plus, the pot likker (another essential Southern food), the liquid produced when braising them, retains most of the nutrition leached from the leaves—another reason to dip your cornbread in it! Be sure to remove the stems, mainly closer to the bottom of the leaf, as they can get very thick and fibrous, especially if you are not braising them and are using them in a quickly cooked dish.

FERMENTED BLACK BEANS

This common Chinese ingredient is produced when soybeans are salted and left to ferment, naturally bringing out a depth of flavor robust with salty, umami-rich notes that are especially great with pork, shellfish, or even octopus. If they come packed in salt, tame their salinity by soaking them in water for at least thirty minutes before using. Store the beans tightly sealed in your refrigerator to extend their lifespan and prevent them from drying out.

FISH SAUCE

Fish sauce is produced when tiny fish (usually anchovies) are salted, fermented in the sun, then pressed to extract the umami-rich liquid that results. I think of it as similar to soy sauce, but with a stronger umami impact, despite it having a lighter visual finish (I personally like to use it in dishes where a darker color is less desired, such as fried rice or light-colored broths). It's great on seafood, in dressings (especially Caesar dressing in place of anchovies), or anywhere you want to raise the level of umami flavor. Look for brands that use the three simple ingredients of fish, salt, and water, like Three Crabs and Red Boat, and store tightly sealed to keep the aroma in the bottle and not throughout your house. I keep it in my pantry, though some refrigerate it.

HAM HOCKS

This staple of Southern cooking is commonly used to flavor the liquid produced when cooking collard greens known as *pot likker*, but this book uses it more often as a primary ingredient in soups and stocks as is the case in the Ham Hock and Daikon Pot Likker (page 94), where the meat is picked from the bones and added back into the pot. Although the ham hock is the joint that attaches the leg to the foot and not known to carry a lot of meat, when cooked low and slow, plenty of meat can be mined, not to mention a ton of rich collagen that gives stocks, soups, and sauces a deliciously lip-smacking quality. Look for ham hocks in grocery stores or at your butcher and make sure they are smoked; in a pinch, substitute bacon, though you will miss the rich collagen boost that ham hocks provide.

HOISIN SAUCE

Used frequently in Chinese, Vietnamese, and Thai cooking, this sweet sauce made from soybeans is dark, thick, sticky, and full of umami, making it great as a marinade or glaze. It's one of the key ingredients in the Char Siu Marinade (page 244), demonstrating how its sweetness and color contribute to the beauty of the final product. A fun way to use it is in place of ketchup in American-style barbecue sauces. My preferred brand is Lee Kum Kee. Refrigerate for up to 6 months after opening—and be sure to get every last bit out of the bottle by swishing with hot water.

LAP CHEONG

Lap cheong is a sweet and salty dried Chinese pork sausage. Used widely in Cantonese cooking along with lap yuk (Chinese bacon), it was traditionally served in cold winter months but is now utilized year-round. Steam it, fry it, grind it for use as a stuffing, or eat it straight from the package. Throwing a few links along with rice in a rice steamer will plump them up and is enough to make a tasty—if humble—meal. Lap cheong will usually be in the refrigerated section of Asian markets, but they can also be kept at room temperature when factory sealed. After opening their package, wrap them tightly and refrigerate for up to 10 days.

MONOSODIUM GLUTAMATE

MSG is a chemical derivative of the naturally occurring glutamate often found in tomatoes, Parmesan cheese, and the kelp known as *kombu*. If you ever wondered what "umami" meant, a couple grains of MSG on your tongue will clear up any confusion. Don't be scared off by the bad rap it got from dubious sources in the last half of the 1900s or by the processed snacks it's often found in; used in moderation—and not as a flavor crutch—MSG boosts the essence of everything's flavor. But remember that less is more with MSG—too much will impart an artificial taste to your food. Fun fact: If you see "accent" listed as an ingredient in things like potato chips, canned soups, condiments, or even spice blends, chances are it's MSG.

OKRA

Okra originally hails from Africa and is now an important ingredient in the Southern larder, brought by enslaved people during the transatlantic slave trade. In the South, we coat it with cornmeal before frying, stew it with tomatoes, or incorporate it into gumbo (the name of which derives from okra's Western African name, *gombo*). But it's not limited to Africa and the South; you can find it wok-fried with sambal in Malaysian cuisine or used as a crudité to dip into a coconut and minced pork dip known as *tao jiao lon* in Thailand. Look for moderately sized pods, as the larger they are, the more fibrous they get. And if you are afraid of okra's mucilaginous qualities, just cook it hot and fast to reduce its slippery nature!

OYSTER SAUCE

Allegedly, oyster sauce was created when Mr. Lee Kum Sheung forgot a pot of oyster soup on the stove, resulting in a thick, salty black sauce that became oyster sauce as we know it today (he'd go on to found Lee Kum Kee sauce company). Oyster sauce is saltier but less sweet than hoisin sauce, made from cooking oysters for hours down to a dark liquid in large basins in the old days. These days, oyster extracts are used to streamline the process. Try it as a flavorful marinade component, or simply drizzle it over ready-to-eat food; oyster sauce is delicious on hot Chinese broccoli. Refrigerate up to 6 months after opening.

RON'S HOLY TRINITY (FRESH GINGER, GREEN ONIONS, GARLIC)

Cajun and Creole cooking have their "holy trinity" of onions, green bell pepper, and celery: an essential aromatic base for myriad dishes. I've got my own holy trinity, a nod to my fellow Southern cooks down toward the Gulf as well as the flavors of my Chinese upbringing: ginger, green onions, and garlic. You'll find these ingredients used together throughout this book, their aromatic qualities adding a distinct flavor to dishes whether they are of Chinese, Southern, or any other origin.

SORGHUM SYRUP

Sorghum is a grain grown for its nutritional content (it can even be popped like popcorn), but Southerners traditionally crush its stalks to make a deeply sweet syrup that can be used as molasses or brown sugar would be. At Lazy Betty, we use it to lacquer our dry-aged ducks, giving them an extra layer of complexity, and it gives a gorgeous sheen to ribs like the Char Siu Glazed Baby Back Ribs (page 110). If you can't find it, honey, molasses, or maple syrup are appropriate substitutes, if with a less beguiling color and flavor. Store at room temperature in an airtight jar indefinitely, and do not refrigerate sorghum syrup, or you'll never get it out of the jar!

STAR ANISE

Star anise is one of the stars of Chinese five-spice powder and one of the key ingredients in Vietnamese pho soup. I often incorporate it whole into stocks and soups or grind it for use as a powder anywhere I want its sweet, licorice flavor (which goes great with the natural sweetness of pork). It was also a key ingredient for the first dish I ever conceptualized at Le Bernardin: poached halibut and baby radishes in a sesame and star anise–infused broth.

SZECHUAN PEPPERCORNS

Floral, tangy, and numbing, Szechuan peppercorns are at times mistaken as being very spicy due to frequent pairing with chiles in the numbing and spicy one-two punch of Szechuan mala seasoning. These anesthetizing peppercorns are one of Chinese cooking's most iconic ingredients. They can be substituted with their Japanese cousin, the sansho peppercorn, which offers a more citrus-forward flavor, but with a heavier price tag. Buy these whole and store in an airtight container for up to one year, then grind as needed to ensure robust flavor.

SHAOXING COOKING WINE

Named after the city in eastern China that it comes from, Shaoxing cooking wine is a rice wine widely used in Chinese stir-fries and braises. Light amber in appearance, it has a mildly sweet flavor. While the version produced for drinking is one of the oldest versions of wine in China, the cheaper cooking variety is only a few decades old and contains salt as an additive. Substitute sweet sherry if unavailable and store Shaoxing cooking wine up to 1 year in a cool, dark place if opened, or indefinitely if unopened.

CHAPTER 1

Vegetables

Betty

My mother is the single biggest influence in my life. She instilled the values that inform how I run my restaurant Lazy Betty, like hard work, inclusivity, and generosity. Time after time, she would welcome friends of family who were often complete strangers to her from all corners of the world, employing them in our restaurant and housing them in our home as they settled in the United States. Many were the times that I had to give up my bedroom and sleep on the couch or scoot over at the dinner table to accommodate these newcomers as we welcomed them into the country that my mom had only recently made home herself. This was beyond Southern hospitality; this was a determination to pay forward the good fortune we'd received, and to help open the door for others to find the same success we'd found.

Today, at my restaurant Lazy Betty, I use the lessons learned from my mother as I strive to employ a diverse crew and utilize ingredients and techniques from many different cultures to find harmony on a plate and among my work family. I'm always grounded by my mother's role as a pioneer in this industry and in this country, applying her life lessons to how I cook and how I run my restaurant as the foundation for finding common ground with others.

LEFT: Ron's mother visiting a garden in San Francisco.

OPPOSITE, CLOCKWISE FROM TOP: Ron's mother shopping; two-year-old Ron in Betty's lap; Betty cutting birthday cake for an employee at Hunan Village.

Stir-Fried Okra

SERVES 2 TO 4 AS AN APPETIZER OR SIDE

A great thing about stir-fries is the ease with which flavor can be quickly imparted not only via aromatic ingredients like garlic and ginger, but through wok hei, aka "dragon breath" (see page 173). Plus, stir-frying is quick, keeping vegetables fresh and vibrant, especially important with something like okra, which becomes overly slimy when cooked slowly.

2 tablespoons canola oil

4 cloves garlic, thinly sliced

1-inch (2.5 cm) piece fresh ginger, peeled and thinly sliced

1 Fresno chile, seeds removed and sliced into thin rounds (optional)

10 basil leaves

12 ounces (340 g) okra, sliced into ¼-inch (6 mm) pieces (about 3 cups)

2 tablespoons Shaoxing cooking wine

2 tablespoons Chicken Stock (page 189)

1 teaspoon toasted sesame oil

Salt and white pepper

In a wok or large sauté pan, heat the canola oil over high heat. When thin wisps of smoke rise from the pan, add the garlic and ginger and cook, stirring frequently (stir-frying) for 10 seconds, or until the aromatics just start to brown. Add the chile, if using, and basil and stir-fry for an additional 10 seconds, or until the basil starts to wilt. Add the okra and stir constantly for about 30 seconds, until the okra becomes bright green. Add the wine and stock and cook for another 15 seconds to let the liquid reduce. Add the sesame oil, season with salt and white pepper, and serve immediately.

Grilled Okra with Mala Oil

SERVES 2 TO 4 AS AN APPETIZER OR SIDE

Common in China, the American South, and Africa, where it originated, okra's relatively strong and sturdy composition makes it a good candidate for cooking over the harsh, high heat of a grill. It can also stand up to assertive flavors, so the addition of mala oil works perfectly as a finishing touch, collecting in okra's ribbed sides, adding a deliciously numbing heat to the crunchy green vegetable.

4 (6-inch / 15 cm) bamboo skewers, soaked in water for at least 10 minutes

16 pieces okra, tops trimmed

Olive oil

Salt and white pepper

2 tablespoons Mala Oil (page 247)

1 tablespoon sliced green onions, green parts only

1 tablespoon chopped cilantro

2 tablespoons crushed toasted peanuts

Prepare a grill for direct medium heat grilling.

Meanwhile, skewer 4 pieces of okra crosswise onto each skewer. Drizzle with olive oil and season with salt and white pepper.

Place on the grill and cook for about 90 seconds, then flip and cook for an additional 90 seconds, until the okra is beginning to char, has become brighter in color, and is becoming tender.

Remove the okra from the skewers, drizzle with the mala oil, and top with the green onions, cilantro, and peanuts. Serve immediately.

Cornmeal-Crusted Fried Chinese Eggplant

SERVES 2 TO 4 AS AN APPETIZER OR SIDE

This recipe sits happily at the confluence of a deliciously numbing Chinese flavor profile with its palate-numbing spiciness of Szechuan peppercorns and a Southern cornmeal crust–frying technique. Serve it with Red Pepper Marmalade (page 243) as an appetizer, or as a side with Pot Roast with Daikon and Shiitake Mushrooms (page 176).

2 Chinese eggplants, skin left on, cut into 3-inch (7.5 cm) wedges (about 1 pound / 455 g total)

Salt

FOR THE EGG WASH:

2 large eggs

1 cup (240 ml) whole milk

FOR THE CORNMEAL CRUST:

2 cups (300 g) coarse cornmeal

1 tablespoon onion powder

1 tablespoon garlic powder

1 tablespoon ginger powder

1 teaspoon salt

FOR THE FINISHING SPICE:

¾ teaspoon ground coriander

1 tablespoon Chinese five-spice powder

1½ teaspoons ground Szechuan peppercorns

¾ teaspoon crushed Szechuan chili flakes (see Notes)

¼ teaspoon sugar

¼ teaspoon MSG (see Notes)

Canola oil, for deep-frying

2 cups (240 g) all-purpose flour

1 tablespoon chopped cilantro

Place the eggplant wedges in a bowl and season with salt, then lay them in a single layer on a paper towel–lined plate. Set aside for 15 minutes to extract excess liquid.

MAKE THE EGG WASH: In a medium bowl, whisk the eggs and milk together thoroughly. Set aside.

MAKE THE CORNMEAL CRUST: In a medium bowl, thoroughly mix the cornmeal, onion powder, garlic powder, ginger powder, and salt. Spread on a baking sheet and set aside.

MAKE THE FINISHING SPICE: In a small skillet, toast the coriander, Chinese five-spice powder, Szechuan peppercorns, and crushed Szechuan chili flakes over medium heat until fragrant, about 1 minute. Transfer to a small bowl and allow to cool, then add the sugar and MSG and stir to combine.

When ready to proceed, set up a frying station. In a large, heavy pot set up with an oil thermometer, heat 2 inches (5 cm) oil over high heat until it reaches 350°F (175°C). Have a spider and a large bowl ready.

Pat the eggplant dry. In a large bowl, toss the eggplant with the flour. Shake off any excess flour, then dip the eggplant in the egg wash and allow the excess to drip off. Roll the dipped eggplant in the cornmeal crust, then place on a baking sheet.

Working in batches as necessary to avoid overcrowding the oil and dropping the oil temperature, gently lay the crusted eggplant in the oil. Fry until golden brown, 4 to 5 minutes, then use a spider to remove the eggplant from the oil, shaking off excess oil, and set in the bowl. Season with the finishing spice, then transfer the eggplant to a serving platter. Sprinkle with chopped cilantro and serve immediately.

NOTES:

Szechuan chili flakes are a moderately spiced chili that provide the deep red color in the Mala Oil on page 247. They also provide a hint of tanginess that you won't get from crushed red chili or gochugaru.

As for MSG, when associated with Chinese food, it's gotten some bad press over the years due to false, xenophobic claims made way back in the sixties. Ironically, no one complains about getting "MSG headaches" when they gorge on processed snack foods loaded with the stuff. I embrace it as a simple seasoning agent that boosts the umami component of a dish when used in moderation just like it is here.

Spring Onion, Garlic Chive, and Zucchini Fritters

SERVES 2 TO 4 AS AN APPETIZER OR SIDE

I can't take full credit for these fritters, as my wife was the one who introduced them to me, frequently making them for our daughter, Calliope, and for me as a snack or dinner side. But since then, I've evolved them by adding more pungent flavors like cilantro, ginger, and Chinese garlic chives since zucchini is so mild. These fritters are a great little snack but also work well next to the Char Siu Glazed Baby Back Ribs (page 110).

3 large eggs

2 cloves garlic, minced

1 tablespoon minced, peeled fresh ginger

1 teaspoon lime zest

1 teaspoon toasted sesame oil

¼ cup (15 g) chopped cilantro

Salt and black pepper

2 cups (250 g) grated zucchini (from 2 to 3 small zucchini), excess moisture wrung out (see Note)

½ cup (110 g) finely shredded cabbage

½ cup (55 g) thinly sliced green onions, green and white parts

½ cup (55 g) Chinese garlic chives, cut into ¼-inch (6 mm) pieces

1 cup (50 g) panko

Canola oil

Red Pepper Marmalade (page 243), for serving

In a large bowl, beat the eggs with the garlic, ginger, lime zest, sesame oil, cilantro, and salt and black pepper to taste. Add the zucchini, cabbage, green onions, garlic chives, and panko and gently mix to combine. Set aside.

In a medium nonstick skillet, heat 2 tablespoons canola oil over medium heat. Carefully drop about 2 tablespoons of the batter into the pan, gently pressing to flatten into a disk. Repeat until the pan is full without any fritters touching. Cook until browned, 1 to 2 minutes, then flip and brown the other side for another 1 to 2 minutes.

Transfer to a plate, sprinkle with salt, and repeat the process until all the batter is used. Serve immediately with the red pepper marmalade alongside.

NOTE:

You want the zucchini to be free of any excess moisture before using it in this recipe. After grating it, place it in the middle of a clean kitchen towel, then gather the four corners of the towel to form a purse holding the zucchini. Twist the top of the towel, forming an ever-tightening ball around the zucchini as you continue to twist, wringing out the excess moisture, which can simply be discarded.

Braised Romaine with Ham Hock Pot Likker

SERVES 2 TO 4 AS AN APPETIZER OR SIDE

This Chinese-style braised romaine will be new to many Western cooks, shining a light on a delicious new facet of the potential of lettuce: cooking it. Rare in the United States, it is very common in Asia, and though I personally hadn't eaten it growing up, it's a favorite of my wife, Jackie, that she was only able to get in Hong Kong, until I devised a recipe for her. The first time I ate the dish myself was when my partner in crime on Netflix's *The Final Table*, Chef Shin Takagi, sent me to a favorite spot, Ming Chú, while I was traveling through Hong Kong. There, they braised lettuce in a clay pot—it was absolutely magical and soon became a favored dish in my repertoire. The secret is cooking the lettuce *just* enough so that it can retain some of its crunch, and pairing it with a meaty, salty liquid to braise in. Here we use our Ham Hock and Daikon Pot Likker (page 94), which perfectly complements the lightness and sweetness of the romaine.

2 tablespoons canola oil

1 romaine lettuce heart, cut in half lengthwise

2 cloves garlic, sliced

1-inch (2.5 cm) piece fresh ginger, peeled and cut into 1 by ⅛ inch (2.5 cm by 3 mm) matchstick strips

½ cup (120 ml) Ham Hock and Daikon Pot Likker (page 94)

Salt and white pepper

In an 11-inch (28 cm) skillet with a tight-fitting lid, heat the oil over medium heat. When thin wisps of smoke rise from the pan, add the romaine to the pan cut side down and sear until browned, about 30 seconds. Add the garlic and ginger to the pan and stir until very aromatic, about 15 seconds. Flip the romaine halves and sear the rounded side until golden brown, about an additional 30 seconds.

Add the pot likker to the pan, cover with the lid, and reduce the heat to low. Let the romaine braise in the covered pan until tender, 3 to 4 minutes. Season with salt and white pepper and serve immediately.

Braised Romaine with Nuoc Cham Caesar

SERVES 2 TO 4 AS AN APPETIZER OR SIDE

Thinking back, my love affair with cooked lettuces really started at Le Bernardin, where we served lightly sautéed romaine hearts with brown butter and lemon on a lobster dish. That laid the groundwork for the dish described in the headnote for Braised Romaine with Ham Hock Pot Likker (page 32), and I've been playing with different versions of cooked lettuces ever since. Back home, I love a cool, crisp Caesar salad, but this warm rendition is a fun take on the classic. Fish sauce as the base for the dressing replaces the usual anchovies because I like the flavor and it's in my pantry far more often. Little Gem lettuces work great here as well. Keep extra nuoc cham Caesar dressing in the fridge to throw on future salads or to use as a dip—once you try it, you'll always want this homemade version around.

FOR THE NUOC CHAM CAESAR DRESSING:

1 clove garlic

1 large egg

1 large egg yolk

1 tablespoon fish sauce

Juice of ½ lemon (1 to 2 tablespoons)

1 teaspoon Worcestershire sauce

1 tablespoon red wine vinegar

¼ cup (25 g) finely grated Parmesan cheese

Salt and white pepper

⅔ cup (165 ml) canola oil

FOR THE ROMAINE:

2 tablespoons canola oil

2 romaine lettuce hearts, halved lengthwise

2 cloves garlic, thinly sliced

1-inch (2.5 cm) piece fresh ginger, peeled and cut into 1 by ¼-inch (2.5 cm by 6 mm) matchstick strips

1 tablespoon Shaoxing cooking wine

2 tablespoons Chicken Stock (page 189)

Salt and white pepper

1 teaspoon toasted sesame oil

MAKE THE NUOC CHAM CAESAR DRESSING: Place the garlic, egg, egg yolk, fish sauce, lemon juice, Worcestershire sauce, vinegar, cheese, and salt and white pepper to taste into a blender and blend until smooth, 10 to 15 seconds. With the blender running, slowly drizzle in the canola oil (if the dressing is getting too thick, add a few drops of water as needed, then proceed with the oil). Adjust the seasoning with salt and white pepper and set aside.

MAKE THE ROMAINE: In a large, lidded skillet, heat 1 tablespoon of the canola oil over medium heat, then place romaine hearts cut side down in the pan and sear to a light golden brown, about 15 seconds. Remove from the pan and set aside.

Add the remaining 1 tablespoon canola oil to the pan and reduce the heat to medium-low. Add the garlic and ginger and cook, stirring constantly to infuse them into the oil, until they are lightly browned, about 15 seconds. Return the romaine hearts to the pan and add the wine and stock and season with salt and white pepper.

Brush each romaine heart with roughly 2 tablespoons of the dressing, cover the pan, reduce the heat to low, and cook until the lettuce is tender, 2 to 3 minutes.

Remove from the heat and brush the sesame oil over each romaine half and serve immediately. Refrigerate any unused dressing in an airtight container for up to 4 weeks.

Stir-Fried Long Beans with Bacon

SERVES 2 TO 4 AS AN APPETIZER OR SIDE

This dish is as much as a staple in Chinese cuisine as green bean casserole is in the American South and is one of the few vegetable-centered dishes that my daughter, Calliope, will willingly eat. Traditionally paired with ground or thin slivers of pork, we make ours with bacon and omit the commonly used dried shrimp and Chinese pickles for simplicity's sake, but if you prefer a traditional version, modify as you like by adding a few dried shrimp alongside the garlic and ginger, or even spice it up by adding a sliced Fresno chile. These bacony beans work in harmony with a bowl of Fundamental Steamed Rice (page 87) for a stand-alone meal, or as one of many communal dishes served in a family-style dinner. If you have trouble finding long beans, green beans are a good substitute.

1 tablespoon grapeseed oil, plus more as needed

3 slices thick-sliced bacon, cut into ¼-inch (6 mm) pieces

1 pound (455 g) long beans, tips trimmed, cut into 1-inch (2.5 cm) lengths

½ cup (80 g) chopped onion

2 cloves garlic, minced

1 teaspoon minced, peeled fresh ginger

1 Fresno chile, thinly sliced on the bias (optional)

1 tablespoon oyster sauce

1 teaspoon soy sauce

Salt and white pepper

In a wok or large skillet, heat the oil over medium-high heat. Add the bacon and cook until the fat begins to render out and the bacon is light golden brown, 1 to 2 minutes. Remove the skillet from the heat, strain the fat from the bacon, and set the bacon aside.

Return 3 tablespoons of the fat to the skillet (if fewer than 3 tablespoons of fat are available, make up the difference with additional oil). Place the skillet back over medium-high heat. When thin wisps of smoke rise from the skillet, add the green beans and cook, stirring occasionally, letting the beans fry and blister for 2 to 3 minutes. Remove the beans from the skillet and set aside.

Place the onion, garlic, ginger, and chile, if using, in the skillet and fry until the vegetables are beginning to soften and color slightly, 1 to 2 minutes.

Return the green beans and bacon to the skillet and cook, stirring occasionally, for about 1 minute to allow the ingredients to marry. Add the oyster sauce and soy sauce and cook, stirring occasionally, for another minute. Season with salt and white pepper and serve immediately.

Crushed Garlic and Cucumber Salad

SERVES 2 TO 4 AS AN APPETIZER, SIDE, OR SMALL MAIN COURSE

This humble salad has been a constant during every stage of my life, from my childhood, where it was a side to many of my meals growing up, to today, where it acts as a ban chan (small side dish) for a Bo Ssam dinner (page 98), a cooling salad to a bowl of spicy wontons, or a condiment not unlike kimchi with Korean barbecue or sauerkraut in a rich Alsatian choucroute garnie. It even inspired a dish of mine at Le Bernardin during my time as creative director, wherein a sashimi-style slice of salmon was paired with a fancy version of this salad, the whole plate dressed with a sauce of cucumber juice, cilantro, and mala oil.

2 green onions, green and white parts chopped

25 cilantro leaves

1 tablespoon apple cider vinegar

1 tablespoon Chinese black vinegar

1 tablespoon toasted sesame oil

1 clove garlic, minced

3 English (seedless) cucumbers

Salt and white pepper

In a large bowl, mix the green onions, cilantro, both vinegars, sesame oil, and garlic to combine and set aside.

Cut the unpeeled cucumbers into ½-inch (12 mm) rounds, then place them into a zip-top plastic bag with a pinch of salt. Seal the bag, pressing out as much air as possible. Using the flat side of a cleaver or large knife, gently but firmly press down on the bag to smash the cucumbers. The goal is to have each round ruptured but still in one piece and not broken into smithereens. Add the crushed cucumbers and their juices to the vinegar mixture and gently toss with your hands or a large spoon, taking care not to bruise the ingredients. Season with salt and white pepper and serve immediately.

Cucumber and Tomato Salad with Mala-Buttermilk Dressing

SERVES 2 TO 4 AS AN APPETIZER, SIDE, OR SMALL MAIN COURSE

This recipe is one of my favorites in this book, a beautiful and refreshing combination of the South's bountiful summer produce and Asian flavors. This is an evolved version of a traditional Crushed Garlic and Cucumber Salad (page 39), adding a rich, tangy buttermilk dressing that cools and balances the spicy mala oil. Smashing the cucumbers opens them up to carry more of the dressing, but take care not to completely demolish them. I suggest using a light Chinese cleaver, which provides a good amount of finesse, as opposed to its heavier Western counterparts.

FOR THE DRESSING:

1 clove garlic, minced

½ teaspoon minced, peeled fresh ginger

1 teaspoon lime zest

½ cup (120 ml) buttermilk (full fat if possible)

FOR THE SALAD:

2 English (seedless) cucumbers

Salt and white pepper

1 cup (150 g) halved cherry tomatoes

¼ cup (4 g) loosely packed mint leaves

¼ cup (4 g) loosely packed cilantro leaves

3 green onions, green and white parts thinly sliced (about ¼ cup / 25 g)

2 tablespoons Mala Oil (page 247), plus more if desired

1 lime, halved

MAKE THE DRESSING: In a medium bowl, whisk the garlic, ginger, lime zest, and buttermilk to thoroughly combine and set aside at room temperature for at least 1 hour to allow the ingredients to marry.

MAKE THE SALAD: Cut the unpeeled cucumbers into ½-inch (12 mm) rounds, then place them into a zip-top plastic bag with a pinch of salt. Seal the bag, pressing out as much air as possible. Using the flat side of a cleaver or large knife, gently but firmly smash the cucumbers. The goal is to have each round ruptured but still in one piece and not broken into smithereens.

Place the crushed cucumbers and their juices into a large bowl and add the tomatoes, mint, cilantro, and green onions and gently toss with your hands or a large spoon. Add the dressing and gently toss again, only enough to distribute the dressing, taking care not to further bruise the ingredients. Season with salt and white pepper and transfer to a shallow serving dish.

Drizzle the salad with the mala oil and finish by squeezing the lime over the dish to finish (doing so earlier could cause the buttermilk to curdle). Serve immediately.

Five-Spice Sorghum-Glazed Carrots with Toasted Pecans

SERVES 2 TO 4 AS AN APPETIZER OR SIDE

This dish holds a special place in my heart because it is a version of one my wife and I had on our first date at the now-closed Breslin by April Bloomfield in New York, and to this day we always order roasted carrots when dining out together. The Chinese five-spice brings out an unexpected side of the carrots, its cinnamon pairing perfectly with the sweetness of the molasses-like sorghum and the carrots themselves, while the pecans add a rich crunch. It's a perfect side for Thanksgiving dinner (or any cold-weather meal, for that matter), and they'd even pair well with a Cantonese-style Peking duck if you were so inclined. Try to use actual baby carrots when possible; their subtle sweetness is far superior to that of the mass produced "baby-cut carrots," which are just huge carrots shaved down to size. If you can't find true baby carrots, use smaller, medium carrots.

1 pound (455 g) baby carrots, peeled and tops removed

2 tablespoons olive oil

1½ teaspoons Chinese five-spice powder

Salt and black pepper

2 tablespoons sorghum syrup

2 tablespoons unsalted butter

½ cup (56 g) chopped pecans

4½ teaspoons lemon juice (about ½ large lemon)

Preheat the oven to 425°F (220°C).

Place the carrots, oil, Chinese five-spice powder, and salt and black pepper to taste in a large bowl and toss to coat carrots. Spread the carrots onto a baking sheet and roast for 10 minutes. Remove the carrots from the oven and drizzle with the sorghum syrup, shaking the pan to distribute the syrup. Return the carrots to the oven and roast until tender, 4 to 5 minutes longer, taking care not to burn the sorghum syrup.

Meanwhile, in a large skillet, melt the butter over low heat. Add the pecans and toast until aromatic and golden brown, 3 to 4 minutes. Remove the carrots from the oven and transfer them and any accumulated juices into the pan with the pecans. Add the lemon juice and gently toss all of the ingredients together, then place in a serving bowl and serve immediately.

Hoisin-Roasted Eggplant

SERVES 2 TO 4 AS AN APPETIZER OR SIDE

I love eggplant. It's one of the few vegetables that has such a strong identity within the country it derives from, be it China, Japan, or Italy, and can feel completely distinct from dish to dish—just think of the differences between baba ghanoush, eggplant Parmesan, and eggplant caponata. This dish is a bit of a mash-up, as oven-roasted eggplant is rare in Asian cuisine. Plus, we're using an Italian eggplant—if you can find a beautiful, speckled Fairy Tale eggplant, all the better. Note that dark soy sauce gives the finished eggplant a beautiful, deep-amber lacquer, but in a pinch, standard soy sauce will work just fine.

1 small (10-ounce / 280 g) Italian eggplant

2 tablespoons sorghum syrup

1 teaspoon Shaoxing cooking wine

1 tablespoon dark soy sauce

1½ teaspoons toasted sesame oil

¼ cup (60 ml) hoisin sauce

¼ cup (60 ml) olive oil

1 teaspoon toasted sesame seeds

2 green onions, green parts only, sliced on the bias

Preheat the oven to 400°F (205°C).

Cut the eggplant in half lengthwise, then score the cut side with ¼-inch (6 mm) wide incisions. Rotate the eggplant 90 degrees and score again to create a crosshatch pattern. Trim a thin strip off the opposite side so the eggplant can sit flat with the scored side up. Set aside.

In a small bowl, mix the sorghum syrup, wine, soy sauce, sesame oil, and hoisin sauce until combined. Set aside.

In a large skillet, heat the olive oil over medium heat. When the oil starts to shimmer, place the eggplant halves scored side down and apply gentle pressure on top for 2 to 3 minutes, until the eggplant is golden brown.

Transfer the eggplant to a baking sheet, scored side up, and generously brush the scored side of the eggplant with the hoisin mixture. Place in the preheated oven and roast until tender, about 15 minutes.

When the eggplant is tender, remove it from the oven and adjust the oven control to broil. Brush the scored side of the eggplant with the hoisin mixture again.

When the broiler is preheated, broil the eggplant for 1 minute. Remove the eggplant from the oven, brush again with the hoisin mixture, and broil for another minute. Repeat this process until there is a nice, thick lacquer on top of the eggplant (if you run out of the hoisin mixture, simply broil the eggplant until the lacquer forms).

Sprinkle with the sesame seeds and green onions and serve immediately.

Persimmon, Arugula, and Pecan Salad with Ginger Vinaigrette

SERVES 2 TO 4 AS AN APPETIZER OR SIDE

I loved persimmons while growing up, but only ate them at home, so I always attributed them to my Asian heritage. Now, as an adult, I find them at local farmers' markets from Georgia to California in the fall, and my Uncle Tony has even dropped freshly picked ones off at our house from his neighborhood persimmon tree. Many cultures celebrate this delicious, mildly sweet, sometimes astringent fruit. This salad enhances the fruit with the peppery heat of arugula and the hearty crunch of Southern pecans, all dressed with a sweet and tangy vinaigrette. For this recipe, look for a non-astringent Fuyu persimmon, which is short and squat with medium-firm flesh when ripe. Avoid the Hachiya variety, which is bit more like a stretched-out acorn, super soft at peak ripeness, and often dried and massaged daily to make the Japanese sweet known as *hoshigaki*.

FOR THE VINAIGRETTE:

1½ teaspoons minced, peeled fresh ginger

3 tablespoons apple cider vinegar

3 tablespoons olive oil

1 tablespoon honey

FOR THE SALAD:

2 cups (40 g) arugula

1 cup (70 g) bok choy leaves, thinly sliced

4 medium carrots, peeled and cut into long ribbons using a peeler (about 2 cups / 220 g)

1 persimmon, halved lengthwise and thinly sliced crosswise

2 tablespoons whole pecans, toasted

Salt and black pepper

MAKE THE VINAIGRETTE: In a small bowl, combine the ginger, vinegar, oil, and honey and whisk until combined. Set aside.

MAKE THE SALAD: In a large bowl, mix the arugula, bok choy, carrots, persimmon, and pecans. Drizzle 3 tablespoons of the vinaigrette over the salad, season with salt and black pepper, and gently toss. Transfer to a serving bowl and serve immediately with additional vinaigrette on the side. Any remaining vinaigrette can be refrigerated for up to 2 weeks.

Curried Cauliflower Soup and Charred Green Onion Relish

SERVES 2 TO 4 AS AN APPETIZER

Like so many fine dining restaurants during the pandemic, Lazy Betty made the temporary move from high-end tasting menus to comforting family-style food for takeout. This vegetarian soup, seemingly rich with curried coconut milk and creamy pureed cauliflower, was a favorite and is actually pretty light. Any perceived richness is balanced with a pop of smoky green, oniony flavor from the relish, which is also great drizzled on a hot steak, over blanched veggies, or even as a hot dog condiment.

FOR THE RELISH:

2 tablespoons canola oil

4 green onions, halved and roots removed

1 clove garlic, minced

2 teaspoons minced, peeled fresh ginger

2 tablespoons chopped cilantro

2 tablespoons olive oil

Salt and white pepper

FOR THE SOUP:

2 tablespoons unsalted butter

2 teaspoons Madras curry powder

1 pound (455 g) cauliflower (about ½ medium), leaves removed and cut into ½-inch (12 mm) pieces

¾ cup (180 ml) milk

¾ cup (180 ml) coconut milk

MAKE THE RELISH: In a large skillet, heat the canola oil over medium-high heat. Add the green onions and cook without stirring until they are lightly browned, about 30 seconds. Add the garlic and ginger and stir constantly to infuse them into the oil until they are lightly browned, about 15 seconds. Transfer to a cutting board and allow to cool slightly.

Roughly chop the green onion mixture and transfer to a bowl, then add the cilantro and olive oil, season with salt and white pepper, and stir well. Set aside.

MAKE THE SOUP: In a medium lidded saucepan, melt the butter over medium-low heat. Add the curry powder and stir for about 1 minute, until fragrant. Add the cauliflower, ¼ cup (60 ml) water, the milk, and coconut milk and bring to a slow simmer. Reduce the heat to maintain a simmer and cook uncovered until the cauliflower is tender, 8 to 10 minutes.

Remove from the heat and puree with an immersion blender until smooth. Taste and season with salt and white pepper.

To serve, ladle the soup into a bowl, top with a drizzle of the relish, and serve immediately. Refrigerate any leftover soup, tightly sealed, for up to 3 days; the relish can be refrigerated for up to 2 weeks.

Stir-Fried Collard Greens with Bacon

SERVES 2 TO 4 AS A SIDE

My parents cooked with Chinese cabbage quite a bit as I was growing up, but they didn't serve collard greens much. When I moved back to Atlanta to open Lazy Betty, I fully embraced this Southern staple, and collards are now a regular item in my fridge at home. They are one of the most versatile vegetables, from traditional braised collards to raw collard salads to quick stir-fries like this one, which offers dynamic textures from the tender leaves to the crunchy stems. I can easily polish off this whole recipe with a bowl of Fundamental Steamed Rice (page 87), but they work great as an accompaniment to Grilled Salmon with Hoisin Barbecue Sauce (page 130), among many other dishes in this book.

1 tablespoon canola oil

2 slices thick-sliced bacon, cut into ¼-inch (6 mm) pieces

2 cloves garlic, minced

1 tablespoon minced, peeled fresh ginger

1 pound (455 g) collard greens, cleaned and chopped (4 cups loosely packed)

1 tablespoon Shaoxing cooking wine

2 tablespoons Chicken Stock (page 189)

1 teaspoon toasted sesame oil

Salt and white pepper

In a wok or large skillet, heat the canola oil over medium heat. Add the bacon and cook, stirring occasionally, until starting to crisp, about 1 minute.

Remove all but roughly 1 tablespoon of fat from the pan and raise the heat to high. Add the garlic and ginger to the pan, stir for about 15 seconds, until fragrant, then add the collards and stir frequently for about 1 minute, until vibrant green and beginning to wilt.

Add the wine, stock, and sesame oil, stir, and cook for another 15 seconds to reduce the liquid. Season with salt and white pepper and serve immediately.

Asian Pear and Napa Cabbage Slaw

SERVES 2 TO 4 AS A SIDE

This crisp, sweet, and spicy slaw is perfect piled onto a slider made with Char Siu Pulled Pork (page 113) or alongside Buttermilk Fried Chicken (page 194). Allow it a quick ten minutes for the flavors to marry, but don't let it sit for too long so that it can stay fresh and crunchy.

1 medium Asian pear, shredded

¼ cup (40 g) chopped kimchi

2 cups (220 g) shredded napa cabbage

¼ cup (30 g) shredded carrots

2 green onions, white and green parts, cut into 2 by ¼-inch (5 cm by 6 mm) matchstick strips

20 mint leaves

2 tablespoons mayonnaise (preferably Duke's)

Juice of 1 lime (1 to 2 tablespoons)

Salt and white pepper

In a large bowl, combine the pear, kimchi, cabbage, carrots, green onions, mint, mayonnaise, and lime juice, season with salt and white pepper, and mix well. Let sit at room temperature for at least 10 minutes, then serve.

Kimchi and Okra Stew

SERVES 2 TO 4 AS A MAIN COURSE

Despite the absence of smoked meats, shellfish, the Cajun trinity, or roux, this dish has the hearty feel of gumbo or étouffée, with a finishing kick of heat from the kimchi. Served over Fundamental Steamed Rice (page 87), it resembles those classics all the more, blending my French-based training and experience with my Southern upbringing and exposure to Cajun food. Okra isn't widely eaten in Korea, but here, it finds synergy with kimchi, just as it does when used with bold Cajun flavors—and if you want to bring it even closer to the American South, throw in some andouille sausage or shrimp with the okra to cook through.

6 cups (1.4 L) Chicken Stock (page 189)

2 green onions, white parts cut into 1-inch (2.5 cm) pieces, green parts thinly sliced and reserved for garnish

½ cup (60 g) sliced yellow onion

2 star anise pods

1-inch (2.5 cm) piece fresh ginger, peeled and cut into 1 by ⅛-inch (2.5 cm by 3 mm) matchstick strips

2 cloves garlic, thinly sliced

1 cup (150 g) kimchi, strained and juices reserved

8 pieces okra, cut crosswise into ¼-inch (6 mm) rounds

½ package (8 ounces / 225 g) silken tofu, drained and cut into 1-inch (2.5 cm) cubes

1 tablespoon toasted sesame oil

Salt and white pepper

1 large egg per person (optional)

In a 2-quart (2 L) saucepan, combine the chicken stock, green onion whites, sliced onion, star anise, ginger, garlic, and kimchi and bring to a gentle simmer over medium-high heat, then reduce the heat to maintain a simmer and cook for 20 minutes.

Add the okra and tofu, return to a simmer, and cook for another 6 minutes. Add the oil and season with salt and white pepper.

If using eggs, crack them into the pan and simmer for 2 minutes, essentially poaching the eggs so the whites are cooked but the yolks are still a bit runny. Add the reserved sliced green onions and serve immediately.

Stir-Fried Watercress

SERVES 2 TO 4 AS AN APPETIZER OR SIDE

Few aromas are as nostalgic to me as that of garlic and ginger perfuming the air while stir-frying. This recipe has evolved from that childhood love of simple vegetable stir-fries, the watercress bringing an assertive personality that can work as well with nothing more than a bowl of Fundamental Steamed Rice (page 87) as it can as a side to smoked barbecue. All the better if the "dragon's breath" of wok hei (see Note, page 173) joins the party, but don't worry, a large skillet works well, too. Note that this dish yields a delicious pot likker that should be served with the stir-fry or on the side.

2 tablespoons canola oil

2 cloves garlic, minced

1 tablespoon minced, peeled fresh ginger

12 ounces (340 g) watercress, washed and dried

2 tablespoons Shaoxing cooking wine

¼ cup (60 ml) Chicken Stock (page 189)

1 teaspoon toasted sesame oil

Salt and white pepper

In a medium wok or large skillet, heat the canola oil over high heat. Add the garlic and ginger and stir constantly to infuse them into the oil until they are lightly browned, taking care not to burn them, about 10 seconds. Add the watercress and cook, stirring frequently (stir-frying), until bright green and beginning to wilt, about 30 seconds. Add the wine and stock and stir-fry until the watercress is wilted, about another 30 seconds. Stir in the sesame oil, season with salt and white pepper, then strain the greens, reserving the liquid.

Transfer the greens to a shallow bowl and serve the reserved liquid on the side to drink or pour over rice.

Watercress Pot Likker

SERVES 2 TO 4 AS A SIDE

This is another take on classic Southern-style collard green pot likker (see Collard Greens with Lap Yuk (Chinese Bacon) Pot Likker, page 93), utilizing flavorful watercress and the nostalgic aroma of ginger that filled our kitchen while I was growing up. The sesame oil and rice vinegar bring the dish even closer to the Chinese American kitchen of my youth; serve this pot likker alongside some Fundamental Steamed Rice (page 87) to round out the experience.

2 tablespoons canola oil

½ cup (60 g) sliced yellow onion

3 cloves garlic, thinly sliced

1-inch (2.5 cm) piece fresh ginger, peeled and sliced ¼ inch (6 mm) thick

2 quarts (2 L) Chicken Stock (page 189)

1 pound (455 g) watercress, washed well and roughly chopped

3 tablespoons rice vinegar

1 teaspoon toasted sesame oil

Salt and white pepper

Place the canola oil in a medium saucepan over medium heat. Add the onion, garlic, and ginger and cook, stirring frequently, until the onion becomes translucent but does not brown, 2 to 3 minutes. Add the stock and bring to a boil, then add the watercress and reduce the heat to maintain a low simmer. Cook until the watercress is tender, 5 to 7 minutes, then remove from the heat and stir in the vinegar and sesame oil and season with salt and white pepper. Serve immediately.

Kimchi Pot Likker

SERVES 2 TO 4 AS A SIDE

My favorite pickle on the planet is kimchi—I love it in stir-fries, soups, or in its purest form as a pickle alongside whatever I'm eating. In Atlanta and the surrounding areas, we're lucky to have a large Korean and Korean American population and many shops that sell kimchi. My favorite is P N Rice Cake House on Buford Highway, where my friend chef Grace Yu sells me bulk jars for my family (for more on the Buford Highway see page 124). Here, we incorporate it into a Southern-style pot likker that can be enriched with the Chinese rice cakes described in the Barbecue Brisket and Rice Cake Stir-Fry recipe (page 172), or simply poach an egg in the broth when done cooking and sop it all up with some Lap Cheong Cornbread (page 120).

2 quarts (2 L) Chicken Stock (page 189)

1½ cups (225 g) kimchi and juice

2 cups (220 g) chopped napa cabbage (1-inch / 2.5 cm pieces)

2 cloves garlic, thinly sliced

1-inch (2.5 cm) piece fresh ginger, peeled and sliced ¼ inch (6 mm) thick

2 green onions, green and white parts, sliced into 1-inch (2.5 cm) pieces

1 teaspoon toasted sesame oil

¼ cup (60 ml) apple cider vinegar

2 tablespoons fish sauce

Combine all the ingredients in a large saucepan over high heat and bring to a boil. Reduce the heat to maintain a low simmer and cook for 1 hour to infuse the flavors. Serve immediately.

CHAPTER 2

Rice

Lazy Betty

Lazy Betty, now in our newer, second home in the Midtown neighborhood of Atlanta, Georgia, is my restaurant that I run with my business partner, Chef Aaron Phillips (who came with me from New York) and Chef de Cuisine Austin Goetzman (who has been with us since our early pop-up days). The name is a tongue-in-cheek reference to my late mother, Betty, who, as the matriarch of an empire of Chinese restaurants named Hunan Village that she built from the ground up, was anything but lazy. We just received our first Michelin star while writing this book, and as proud as she would be of us for that accomplishment, I know that what would really make her beam is our deep commitment to the principles of hospitality that she instilled in me so many years ago.

Culturally at Lazy Betty, we curate an environment to make both staff and guests feel like a part of our family. We believe in pay equality

and pursue it via our unique wage model to close the historically large pay gap between the front and back of house staff. A motto is "impact over income," and we aim to make that impact with our food and beverage, our service, and our treatment of one another. I like to paint this picture to my staff by asking them to imagine having a fancy uncle. This uncle just happens to have a world-class culinary staff and an impeccable sense of service in a beautiful setting, where guests—no matter their background—can revel in the luxury, as family, while under our roof. This is my interpretation of *Southern hospitality*, and we strive to impart it every moment and for every diner at Lazy Betty.

Meanwhile, since the early days of my career, I've been out in the world, gathering experience, technique, and understanding of ingredients outside of my native Georgia. Now, I've brought that experience back to Atlanta, and though I'm running a Michelin-starred fine-dining restaurant, every service, every dish is rooted in the lessons my mother taught me back in the kitchens of Hunan Village.

Likewise, this book is influenced by everything in my life that has come before it. But it has its own unique identity. This isn't a Chinese cookbook, nor is it a fine dining cookbook. It's a cookbook putting on display where I came from, what I've learned since, and who I am as a cook. I won't ask you to employ (many) of the elevated techniques that we use at Lazy Betty; this is a cookbook about what I cook at home with my family, meant for you to share with yours.

OPPOSITE: Ron (center) prepping with executive chef and partner Aaron Phillips (right) and sous chef Bryce Hardison (left).

ABOVE: Lazy Betty's private dining room (top); the main dining room (second from top); a seasonal pasta dish on Lazy Betty's tasting menu (third from top); and a spread of snacks that start off the tasting menu (bottom).

Ron's Asian Southern Dirty Rice

SERVES 2 TO 4 AS A MAIN COURSE

Dirty rice is a simple, comforting Louisiana staple packed with flavor, typically made with the "holy trinity" of onion, celery, and peppers, plus ground meat and/or sausage. In this easy rice cooker dish, we use my own holy trinity (ginger, green onions, and garlic) as well as sweet Chinese sausage. Being a Georgian, I add store- (or farm stand–) bought boiled peanuts for their soft texture; canned roasted peanuts, if a bit crunchier, will work just as well, as they'll soften up a bit as they steam with the rice. I like serving this rice with Lemongrass Pork Chops (page 104).

- 1½ cups (280 g) jasmine rice or other long-grain rice, rinsed and drained
- 2 cups (480 ml) Chicken Stock (page 189)
- 2 links (1½ ounces / 43 g each) lap cheong (Chinese sausage, see page 18), quartered lengthwise and sliced ¼ inch (6 mm) thick
- ½ cup (75 g) boiled peanuts or roasted peanuts, shelled
- 2 star anise pods
- 1 cinnamon stick
- 1 tablespoon canola oil
- 4 cloves garlic, minced
- 1 tablespoon minced ginger
- 2 green onions, green and white parts, finely chopped
- 1 tablespoon soy sauce
- 2 teaspoons toasted sesame oil
- 1 tablespoon sorghum syrup
- Salt and white pepper
- ¼ cup (4 g) cilantro leaves

In the bowl of a rice cooker (see Note), combine the rice, stock, lap cheong, peanuts, star anise, and cinnamon.

In a small skillet, heat the canola oil over medium-low heat. Add the garlic, ginger, and green onions and cook, stirring frequently, until translucent and not browned, about 2 minutes. Add the garlic mixture to the rice cooker and stir to combine. Cook the rice as the manufacturer directs. When finished, let the rice sit for 15 minutes, or until the rice has fully absorbed all the water and is plump and tender.

Meanwhile, in a small bowl, stir the soy sauce, sesame oil, and sorghum syrup to combine.

When the rice has finished cooking, pour the soy sauce mixture into the hot rice and gently stir to combine. Season with salt and white pepper, then garnish with the cilantro and serve immediately.

NOTE:

If you don't have a rice cooker, replace the first two steps as follows: Heat the canola oil in a heavy medium saucepan over medium-low heat, add the garlic, ginger, and green onions and cook, stirring frequently, until translucent and not browned, about 2 minutes. Stir in the rice, stock, lap cheong, peanuts, star anise, and cinnamon and raise the heat to high. When the water boils, reduce the heat to low to maintain a simmer and cover the pot with aluminum foil and a lid. Cook for 11 minutes, then remove from the heat and proceed with the final two steps of the recipe.

Hainanese Chicken Rice Rice

SERVES 4 TO 6 AS A SIDE

This is my version of just the rice component of the famous Hainanese chicken rice, wherein a chicken is gently poached, creating a light broth in which rice is cooked. The chicken is sliced and placed atop the rice, usually accompanied by various vegetables and sauces—but the rich rice cooked in chicken fat is arguably the best part. For this simplified rice-only recipe, it's important to use the chicken fat called for if you can—simply save it as directed when making the Chicken Stock (page 189). This rice is great on its own but works well as a base to which you can add whatever preparation of chicken that you like. Personally, I think the crispy version of the Soy-Braised Chicken (page 186) is an excellent accompaniment.

2 tablespoons chicken fat from Chicken Stock (page 189) or canola oil

2 cloves garlic, minced

2 cups (370 g) jasmine rice or other long-grain rice, rinsed

2¾ cups (660 ml) Chicken Stock (page 189)

2 pandan leaves (see Note, page 256)

2 star anise pods

1-inch (2.5 cm) piece fresh ginger, peeled and cut into 4 thick slices

In a medium saucepan, heat the chicken fat or canola oil over medium heat. Add the garlic and cook, stirring constantly, just until it begins to brown, 15 to 30 seconds. Add the rice and stir for 2 minutes, coating each grain with the fat in the pan. Add the stock, pandan leaves, star anise, and ginger and cover tightly with aluminum foil. When you feel bubbles boiling against the foil (about 2 minutes), reduce the heat to maintain a simmer.

Cook, steaming the rice, until tender, 8 to 10 minutes, then remove from the heat and let rest for 20 minutes. Fluff with a fork and serve immediately.

Asian Delight (Rice Pilaf Perfumed with Chinese Sausage and Poultry Fat)

SERVES 2 TO 4 AS A MAIN COURSE

Rich claypot rice dishes originating in China's Guangdong Province inspired me to make this dish at Le Bernardin for my fellow cooks. I would make my version, dubbed "Asian Delight" by our sous chef, for the team after a long day (and night) of cooking delicate, world-class dishes. At that point, you just want something rich and tasty, and if it's simple, all the better. This rice is all of that, especially if you are lucky enough to have an abundant supply of foie gras fat lying around, which takes this dish to a whole other level. If your household supply of this luxurious ingredient is low, chicken fat reserved from another recipe, like Chicken Stock (page 189), is an excellent substitution.

2 tablespoons chicken fat from Chicken Stock (page 189) or foie gras fat

2 cloves garlic, thinly sliced

2 cups (370 g) jasmine rice or other long-grain rice, rinsed and drained

3 cups (720 ml) Chicken Stock (page 189)

4 links (1½ ounces / 43 g each) lap cheong (Chinese sausage, see page 18), cut crosswise into 1-inch (2.5 cm) pieces

2 star anise pods

1 bay leaf

3 cilantro stems and ½ cup (8 g) cilantro leaves

Salt and white pepper

Fried eggs (optional, see Notes)

Soy sauce

1 tablespoon lime juice (roughly ½ lime)

In a 2-quart (2 L) lidded saucepan (see Notes), heat the fat over medium-low heat. Add the garlic and stir constantly to lightly brown and infuse it into the fat, about 30 seconds. Add the rice to the pan, still stirring constantly, to toast it in the fat until a translucent coating forms around each grain of rice, 2 to 3 minutes. Stir in the stock, sausage, star anise, bay leaf, and cilantro stems.

Cover the pan tightly and increase the heat to high to bring the stock to a boil, then reduce the heat to low and allow the rice to steam for 10 minutes. Remove the pan from the heat and allow the rice to sit, covered, for another 20 minutes, or until the rice has fully absorbed the water and is plump and tender.

Fluff the rice with a fork and remove the star anise, bay leaf, and cilantro stems. Fold in the cilantro leaves and season with salt and white pepper.

Transfer to individual plates and top each serving with a fried egg, if using. Drizzle with soy sauce and lime juice and serve immediately.

NOTES:

If you don't have a lidded saucepan, use aluminum foil fitted tightly around the pan. To gauge if the stock is boiling, simply feel the top of the foil for vibrations from the bubbles and steam rising from the pot.

A fried egg with a runny yolk on top of this rice is an easy, delicious upgrade. I like cooking eggs over high heat to emulate a super-hot wok, which causes the eggs to "souffle" and bubble up, getting crispy and caramelized—my preferred way of eating a fried egg. Just heat a couple tablespoons of canola oil in a small nonstick pan over high heat for 1 to 2 minutes, until smoking, crack an egg into the pan, and allow to cook and bubble up, using a spoon to constantly baste the egg with the excess oil in the pan for 1 to 1½ minutes. Season with salt and white pepper and place on top of the rice.

Collard Green Fried Rice

SERVES 1 TO 2 AS A SMALL ENTRÉE OR SIDE

Growing up, we would use leafy greens like chopped Chinese broccoli, cabbage, or bok choy in fried rice, but returning to the South after living in New York City, collard greens seemed to be a more natural (and regional) choice. I love the different textures the leaves and the stems provide, and collards are generally cheaper than most of the aforementioned vegetables.

2 tablespoons canola oil

2 cloves garlic, minced

1 teaspoon minced, peeled fresh ginger

1 large egg

2 cups (316 g) leftover jasmine rice or other long-grain rice, cold (see Note)

⅓ pound (150 g) collard greens, cleaned and cut into rough 1-inch (2.5 cm) pieces (1½ cups loosely packed)

2 tablespoons Shaoxing cooking wine

1 teaspoon toasted sesame oil

Salt and white pepper

In a wok or large sauté pan, heat the canola oil over medium-high heat. Add the garlic and ginger and stir constantly to infuse them into the oil until they are lightly browned, about 15 seconds.

Crack the egg into the pan and quickly scramble for about 10 seconds, until the curds just begin to form, then add the rice and stir, gently smashing the rice so that any clumps are broken up. Continue to cook, stirring frequently, for another 2 minutes, or until the egg is almost cooked through but is still moist.

Add the collard greens, wine, and sesame oil and cook for another minute, or until the greens are wilted. Season with salt and white pepper and serve immediately.

NOTE:

Fried rice is a fantastic use for cold, leftover rice; I like to toss day-old rice with a bit of canola oil (about 1 teaspoon of oil per cup of rice) before adding it to the pan to ensure the rice breaks up and stir-fries evenly.

Garlic Fried Rice with Chicken Fat

SERVES 1 TO 2 AS A SIDE

This fried rice is inspired by the delicious Filipino garlic fried rice, sinangag, introduced to me by my Filipina girlfriend way back when I was in culinary school in Australia (sorry, Jackie!). Lightly browning the garlic in chicken fat really brings the savory richness, but if you don't have chicken fat lying around, use canola oil. Note that chicken fat will smoke and burn a bit quicker than oil, so be prepared and work quickly, but be sure the garlic is lightly browned before adding more ingredients. Eat this fried rice on its own with a bit of kimchi, or as a welcome side car to pretty much any entrée—it's a lot of garlic, but it's totally worth it.

2 tablespoons canola oil

4 large cloves garlic, minced

½ cup (50 g) thinly sliced green onions, white to light green parts

1 large egg

2 cups (316 g) leftover jasmine rice or other long-grain rice, cold (see Note, page 73)

2 tablespoons Shaoxing cooking wine

1 teaspoon toasted sesame oil

Salt and white pepper

In a wok or large sauté pan, heat the canola oil over medium-high heat. Add the garlic and stir constantly to infuse it into the oil until it is lightly browned, about 15 seconds. Add the green onions and cook for another 10 seconds.

Crack the egg into the pan and quickly scramble for about 10 seconds, then add the rice and stir, gently smashing it so that any clumps are broken up. Continue to cook, stirring frequently, for another 2 minutes.

Add the wine and sesame oil and cook for another minute, or until the flavors marry and the rice is heated through. Season with salt and white pepper and serve immediately.

Kitchen Sink Fried Rice

SERVES 1 TO 2 AS A SIDE

Now that I'm a father and husband, I make this dish probably once a week for a quick healthy meal that does a good job of hiding veggies from my six-year-old daughter and lets me spend more time with my family and less time in the kitchen cooking! Double the recipe for leftovers, something I often do, packing it for her school lunch the next day. As its name implies, this fried rice is loaded with whatever might be lying around your kitchen. I've included common ingredients usually found in my home pantry, but if you have other things you'd like to use, such as celery, snow peas, or asparagus (or even hot dogs!), feel free to add them in place of or in addition to the ingredients listed. As far as ratios go, I tend to use a lot more veggies and protein here compared to my other fried rice recipes, but adjust amounts as you see fit and even drizzle in some soy sauce at the end of the cooking process to bump up flavor as desired. In my other fried rice recipes (see pages 73–74), I include a splash of Shaoxing cooking wine to help loosen and re-steam the cold rice, but in this dish there's enough liquid from the veggies and kimchi.

2 tablespoons canola oil

2 slices thick-sliced bacon, cut into ¼-inch (6 mm) pieces

1 large egg

2 cloves garlic, minced

2 tablespoons finely chopped green onion, white and green parts

¼ cup (30 g) chopped carrot

¼ cup (30 g) chopped onion

¼ cup (30 g) frozen peas, thawed

2 cups (316 g) leftover jasmine rice or other long-grain rice, cold (see Note, page 73)

½ cup (75 g) chopped kimchi

4 ounces (115 g) collard greens, cleaned and chopped (1 cup loosely packed)

1 tablespoon toasted sesame oil

Salt and white pepper

In a wok or large sauté pan, heat the canola oil over medium-high heat. Add the bacon and stir to brown it for 20 to 30 seconds.

Crack the egg into the pan and quickly scramble for about 10 seconds, until curds just begin to form, then add the garlic, green onion, carrot, onion, and peas, stirring for another 15 seconds, or until the eggs look like slightly undercooked scrambled eggs.

Add the rice and cook, gently smashing it so that any clumps are broken up and stirring for another 2 minutes.

Add the kimchi, collard greens, and sesame oil and cook for an additional minute, or until the flavors marry and the rice is heated through. Season with salt and white pepper and serve immediately. Refrigerate any extra in an airtight container for up to 3 days. When reheating, sprinkle a few drops of water over the rice to help re-steam it, cover tightly, and microwave until hot.

Claypot Rice with Okra and Smoked Ham Hocks

SERVES 2 TO 4 AS A MAIN COURSE

I first discovered traditionally prepared claypot dishes while living in New York's Chinatown during my Le Bernardin days. I stumbled into a hole in the wall restaurant specializing in them and ordered one rich with savory Chinese sausage and earthy shiitake mushrooms and was immediately hooked. What I loved, and later realized wasn't just a gimmick, was the heavy clay pot the dish was served in, which kept all the flavor and heat contained in a single vessel from stove to table and created a deliciously crispy layer of rice to be discovered when the bottom of the pot was reached. If you don't have a traditional Chinese style claypot, you can you use dolsot (a Korean stone bowl) or a Dutch oven. This version brings a deep, smoky richness from the pot likker, perfect on a chilly evening.

½ cup (120 ml) liquid plus ½ cup (120 g) ham hock meat from Braised Romaine with Ham Hock Pot Likker (page 32)

2 cups (370 g) jasmine rice or other long-grain rice, rinsed and drained

2 tablespoons canola oil

1 tablespoon sorghum syrup

1 tablespoon soy sauce

1 tablespoon oyster sauce

½ teaspoon toasted sesame oil

1 clove garlic, thinly sliced

½-inch (12 mm) piece fresh ginger, peeled and cut into ½ by ¼-inch (12 mm by 6 mm) matchstick strips

2 star anise pods

4 pieces okra, cut into ¼-inch (6 mm) rounds

2 green onions, green parts only, thinly sliced

In a medium saucepan, bring the liquid from the pot likker and 1½ cups (360 ml) water to a boil over high heat, then remove from the heat and set aside.

In a large Chinese claypot, Korean stone bowl, or Dutch oven, mix the rice and canola oil. Place over medium heat, stir, and warm the pot for 1 minute. Add the hot pot likker to the rice, then remove from the heat and let the pot sit for 1 hour.

Meanwhile, in a small bowl, mix the sorghum syrup, soy sauce, oyster sauce, and sesame oil and set aside.

When ready to proceed, add the garlic, ginger, star anise pods, and ¼ cup (60 ml) water, cover, place over low heat, and cook for 5 minutes. Add the ham hock meat, okra, and green onions to the pot without stirring, cover, and cook for another 5 minutes.

Remove the lid, increase the heat to medium, and cook until the bottom of the rice is crisped, about 3 minutes. Drizzle the sorghum mixture over the rice, stir, and serve immediately.

Sticky Rice with Ham Hocks, Peanuts, and Dates

SERVES 4 TO 6 AS A MAIN COURSE

Whenever I eat dim sum, I go straight for the sticky rice wrapped in bamboo leaves, summoning memories of my Aunt Nancy's proficiency wrapping them. She was the only one of my mother's seven siblings who could properly wrap them, and with Aunt Nancy around, I could always count on these morsels of sticky, chewy rice appearing. Here, we steam a big batch of the rice without leaves, with shiitake mushrooms bringing a strong earthiness while grounding the rich sausage and moist ham hocks wonderfully. Texturally, the dates add a sweet and soft element, and the peanuts add a crunchy richness. Look for short-grain rice labeled "glutinous," which will cook up intentionally sticky and dense, but despite its name contains no gluten.

2 tablespoons soy sauce

3 cups (660 g) short-grain glutinous rice, rinsed 3 times and soaked in cold water for at least 3 hours, drained

½ cup (75 g) roasted peanuts

5 Medjool dates, pitted and chopped

1 tablespoon toasted sesame oil

3 tablespoons canola oil

½ cup (80 g) chopped onion

1 tablespoon minced ginger

2 cups (170 g) chopped shiitake mushrooms (stems removed)

2 links (1½ ounces / 43 g each) lap cheong (Chinese sausage, see page 18), halved lengthwise and sliced ¼ inch (6 mm) thick

1 tablespoon oyster sauce

2 ounces (55 g) ham hock meat from Smoked Ham Hock and Seaweed Soup (page 118, see Note)

Salt and white pepper

1 green onion, green part only, thinly sliced

30 cilantro leaves

In a rice cooker, place 3 cups (720 ml) water and 1 tablespoon of the soy sauce and stir to combine. Add the drained rice, peanuts, and dates, making sure everything is evenly distributed, then cook the rice as the manufacturer directs. Once the rice is done, drizzle the sesame oil over the rice and use chopsticks to gently but thoroughly distribute the oil, taking care to not break up the rice.

In a large nonstick skillet, heat 2 tablespoons of the canola oil over medium heat. Add the onions, ginger, mushrooms, and sausage to the pan and cook without browning, stirring occasionally, for 8 to 10 minutes. Add the oyster sauce and remaining 1 tablespoon soy sauce to the pan and continue to cook, slightly reducing the liquid, for about 1 minute, then transfer the hot ingredients to a medium bowl and allow to cool.

Return the empty pan to the heat and add the remaining 1 tablespoon canola oil. Add the cooked rice to the pan and cook, stirring frequently (stir-frying), making sure the rice doesn't burn or stick while breaking it up until heated through, about 4 minutes. Add the cooked sausage mixture back to the pan along with the ham hock meat, if using.

Continue to stir-fry until the ingredients have mixed together and are heated through, 2 to 3 minutes. Adjust the seasoning with salt and white pepper, then add the green onions and cilantro to the pan, stir one more time, and serve immediately.

NOTE:

If you don't have the ham hocks handy, simply omit them and double the amount of lap cheong used.

Bacon Congee and Poached Eggs

SERVES 2 AS A MAIN COURSE

The savory rice porridge known across Asia as congee was (and still is) one of my favorite breakfast staples. Once a week, my mom would make congee, the base product intentionally left bland as a blank canvas to be loaded with varying flavorful accompaniments. My favorite back then consisted of scrambled eggs, sweet pork floss (see Note), and enough soy sauce to make the congee as brown as barbecue sauce. These days, I favor the one-pot ease of poaching the eggs directly in the congee, and my adult palate prefers a more finessed approach to flavoring, using just enough soy sauce to season the porridge, richly aromatic sesame oil, crunchy peanuts, the bright punch of kimchi and green onions, and, of course, plenty of that pork floss I grew to love as a child.

1 tablespoon canola oil

6 pieces thick-sliced bacon, cut into 1-inch (2.5 cm) pieces

⅔ cup (125 g) jasmine rice or other long-grain rice, rinsed and drained

6 cups (1.4 L) Chicken Stock (page 189), or water

Salt and white pepper

4 large eggs

SUGGESTED ACCOMPANIMENTS:

2 tablespoons soy sauce

2 tablespoons toasted sesame oil

¼ cup (40 g) roasted peanuts

¼ cup (40 g) kimchi

2 tablespoons thinly sliced green onions, green parts only

¼ cup (17 g) pork floss (see Notes)

In a medium saucepan, heat the canola oil over low heat. Add the bacon and cook until the fat is rendered and the bacon is beginning to crisp, 4 to 6 minutes. Discard most of the fat from the pan, leaving at most 1 tablespoon.

Stir in the rice and stock and raise the heat to high to bring to a boil, then reduce the heat to maintain a low simmer. Cook to a porridge-like consistency, 45 minutes to 1 hour, stirring frequently so the congee doesn't burn on the bottom of the pot and adding liquid as needed to adjust the consistency to your liking (see Notes). Season the congee with salt and white pepper, keeping in mind that the accompaniments you choose to add will play a role in seasoning as well.

When congee is done, crack the eggs directly into the saucepan, evenly distributing them to ensure separation, and cover with a lid or aluminum foil. Poach until the egg whites are cooked through but yolk is still runny, 6 to 7 minutes.

Portion the congee and eggs into two bowls, making sure not to break the egg yolks, and serve immediately with your desired accompaniments.

NOTES:

Pork floss, easily found in Asian markets or online, is the sweet and salty result of pork being slowly braised, dried, and fried, giving it an almost cotton candy–like consistency. Give it a try, it's pretty addictive.

Speaking of consistency, make your congee as thick or thin as you like, just as you would with oatmeal or other porridges. I like mine just a bit soupier than a typical bowl of oatmeal, giving the accompaniments the chance to really mix into the bowl.

Crispy Rice Sticks with Sriracha Ranch

SERVES 4 TO 6 AS AN APPETIZER OR SNACK

My first chef mentor, Sheri Davis of the now-closed restaurant Dish in Atlanta's Virginia Highlands neighborhood, taught me that the most important way to cook is with lots of heart and emotion, whether building a kitchen team in a restaurant, conceptualizing a dish for a menu, or simply making dinner for loved ones. Food is always better when you prepare it with care—even if that means you are a chef in a restaurant cooking for strangers on Christmas! Cooking with heart means realizing that food can be so much more than just a form of sustenance. And Chef Sheri's lesson has never left me.

Neither has the technique for these rice sticks, something I learned in her kitchen way back when I was a fresh-faced twenty-three-year-old. She paired them with a seaweed salad and seared tuna, but I love them simply as a snack, dipped in the spicy sriracha ranch dressing. Cook the rice as you would risotto, adding a small amount of water at a time while you stir and coax the thickening starch from the rice until just a bit past al dente. The ranch is easy to make, but you could use store-bought if you want; just doctor it up with a bit of sriracha and lime. Serve these rice sticks to your guests at your next Super Bowl party or dinner party. They are also great with the Red Pepper Marmalade (page 243).

FOR THE RICE:

2 cups (440 g) glutinous short-grain rice

1 tablespoon rice vinegar

½ teaspoon sugar

Salt

FOR THE SRIRACHA RANCH:

½ cup (120 ml) mayonnaise (preferably Duke's)

3 tablespoons buttermilk

Zest and juice of 1 lime (1 teaspoon zest and 2 tablespoons juice)

2 tablespoons chopped dill

1 tablespoon sriracha

½ teaspoon crushed black peppercorns

2 tablespoons thinly sliced chives

1 clove garlic, minced

Salt

Canola oil

Place the unrinsed rice in a medium saucepan and add 3 cups (720 ml) water, the vinegar, sugar, and a pinch of salt. Place the pot over medium-high heat and bring to a simmer while stirring. The rice will thicken as it heats and absorbs the water. When most of the water has been absorbed by the rice, after about 5 minutes, add another ¼ cup (60 ml) water and continue to stir until it has been absorbed. Repeat, adding ¼ cup (60 ml) water as needed, roughly every 3 to 5 minutes for a total cooking time of 17 to 20 minutes. You will add a total of about 1 cup (240 ml) additional water during the cooking process. When the rice is just past al dente (like risotto), remove it from the heat and set aside.

Meanwhile, line a 9 by 6-inch (23 by 15 cm) baking sheet with parchment paper. While the rice is still hot, transfer it to prepared tray and spread it so that the rice is in a single layer roughly ½ inch (12 mm) thick. Place another piece of parchment on top of the rice, then place another similar sized baking sheet on top of that paper. Place a couple weights (like tomato cans) on top of the baking sheet and refrigerate to allow the rice to cool down and form into a cohesive, densely packed block, 4 hours to overnight. Remove the rice from the sheet and remove the parchment paper, then cut the rice into 2½ by ½-inch (6 cm by 12 mm) sticks, wiping your knife with a damp towel after each slice. Put the sticks on another parchment-lined baking sheet.

MAKE THE SRIRACHA RANCH: Place the mayonnaise, buttermilk, lime zest and juice, dill, sriracha, peppercorns, chives, garlic and a pinch of salt in a medium bowl and stir to combine. Cover and refrigerate until ready to serve; keep extra refrigerated for up to 1 week.

To cook the rice sticks, heat 3 tablespoons canola oil in a large nonstick skillet over medium heat. Working in batches as necessary, use a spatula or long chopsticks to place the rice sticks into the pan. Cook until browned on one side, 2 to 3 minutes, then flip, repeating this process until the rice sticks are browned on two sides. Place the browned sticks on a paper towel–lined plate and season with salt. When all the rice sticks are cooked, serve them immediately with the sriracha ranch.

Fundamental Steamed Rice

SERVES 2 TO 4 AS A SIDE

My mom showed me how to cook rice with no measurement other than the knuckle of my middle finger, teaching me that it was the perfect water level gauge. Later, a Japanese chef told me the same thing, referring to the knuckle as "Mt. Fuji." I still measure water for rice this way to this day, whether using a rice cooker like my mom did or a pot on the stove top as I learned in culinary school, but we made this recipe a bit more exact for you. Be sure to rinse the rice as directed, which removes the excess starch that can make it gummy.

2 cups (370 g) jasmine rice or other long-grain rice

Place the rice in a medium bowl and cover by 1 inch (2.5 cm) water. Stir the rice about 10 times with your hand, then pour out as much water as possible without pouring out any rice. Repeat this process 2 more times and then fully drain the rice in a colander.

If using a rice cooker, place the rinsed rice and 3 cups (720 ml) water in the cooker and proceed as the manufacturer directs. When done, let the rice rest, covered, for 20 minutes, then fluff with a fork and serve immediately.

If not using a rice cooker, in a heavy medium saucepan, combine the rinsed rice and 3 cups (720 ml) water over high heat. When the water boils, reduce the heat to low to maintain a simmer and cover the pot with aluminum foil and a lid. Cook for 11 minutes, then remove from the heat. Let the rice rest, covered, for 20 minutes, then fluff with a fork and serve immediately.

CHAPTER 3

Pork

Hunan Village

Growing up, our restaurant, Hunan Village, was my home away from home. My mom, with a bribe of Chinese food for my entire sixth grade class, had convinced my school's principal to direct the school bus to drop me off right at the restaurant every day after school as the last stop on the after-school bus route. This arrangement also helped lessen the teasing from the kids on the bus, kids who would mock me with what they perceived to be Chinese-sounding words or accuse my family of serving dog and cat in our restaurant. The restaurant was a place for me to stay out of trouble, where I could finish my homework before getting to work peeling huge fifty-pound bags of onions for two dollars a pop. You're picturing a small Chinese kid sitting on top of bags of onions crying, but believe me, I caught the kitchen work ethic early and loved the experience. I breathed and bled restaurants, and when I decided to make it my career, I flourished, all because of Hunan Village.

Just as importantly, my eyes were opened to the benefit and challenge of the mixing of different cultures. We had Mexican chefs layering Mongolian beef and char siu pork on top of jasmine rice tucked into freshly made tortillas and eating fried rice with intermittent bites of whole fresh jalapeños. They'd make a big batch of arroz con pollo for everyone, onto which the Korean staff would pile kimchi. I was learning how enriching being exposed to other cultures can be.

But I learned about the ugly side of that coin, too, not just from those kids on the bus, but from people who would call the restaurant and ask for "cream of some young guy," cackling as they hung up the phone, as well as the occasional racist remark from a customer in the restaurant. But what stuck with me was my mother's resilience in the face of all of this. She started out much like her staff: not much English, in a foreign country far from home, working long, hard hours to send every penny back home. Who was I to let an ignorant remark bring me down?

OPPOSITE, CLOCKWISE FROM TOP: Waitstaff dressed up for our annual dragon dance at Hunan Village 2 during our Chinese New Year celebration; Ron's cousins and staff after their dragon dance resting in the restaurant; staff from South America and Asia taking a team photo; Ron's siblings, cousins, mother, and grandmother celebrating a birthday at the restaurant.

湖南
Hunan Village II CHINESE
Restaurant

MICHAEL
JACKSON

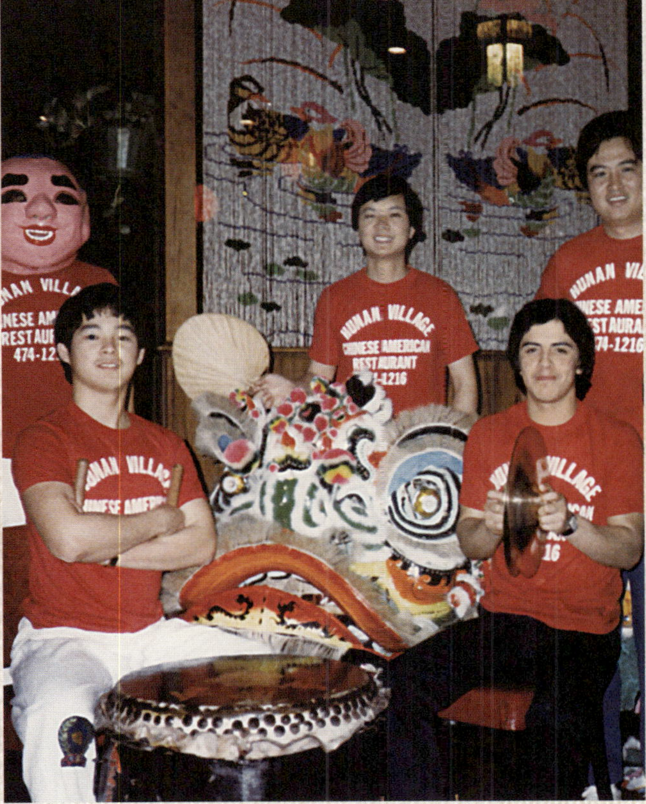
HUNAN VILLAGE
CHINESE AMERICAN
RESTAURANT
474-1216

NIKE

Collard Greens with Lap Yuk (Chinese Bacon) Pot Likker

SERVES 2 TO 4 AS A SIDE

I love having a few packs of lap yuk (Chinese-style bacon) lying around. Cured in soy sauce and Shaoxing cooking wine and either air-dried or smoked, lap yuk offers a sweeter flavor boost than most forms of cured pork. Here, it's used in place of traditional ham hocks to give braised collard greens a complex meatiness rich with star anise and cinnamon. Or just slice it thinly, throw it in with some steaming rice, and finish with a drizzle of soy sauce and a handful of chopped green onions and you have a quick, easy meal. Lap yuk can be found in Chinese markets or online.

2 tablespoons canola oil

½ cup (60 g) sliced yellow onion

3 cloves garlic, thinly sliced

1-inch (2.5 cm) piece fresh ginger, peeled and cut into 1 by ⅛-inch (2.5 cm by 3 mm) matchstick strips

4 ounces (115 g) lap yuk (Chinese bacon), cut crosswise into ¼-inch (6 mm) slices

2 quarts (2 L) Chicken Stock (page 189)

8 ounces (225 g) collard greens, cleaned and chopped (2 cups loosely packed)

¼ cup (60 ml) rice vinegar

Salt and black pepper

Heat the oil in a medium saucepan over medium heat. Add the onion, garlic, and ginger and cook, stirring frequently, until the onion becomes translucent but does not brown, 2 to 3 minutes. Add the lap yuk and stock and bring to a boil. Reduce the heat to maintain a simmer and add the greens.

Cook, stirring occasionally, until the greens become very tender, about 1 hour and 15 minutes. Add the vinegar, season with salt and black pepper, and serve immediately. Refrigerate leftovers in an airtight container for up to 1 week.

Ham Hock and Daikon Pot Likker

SERVES 4 AS A SIDE OR 2 AS A SMALL MAIN COURSE

This dish stems from one I developed during my time at Le Bernardin featuring braised daikon, baby radishes, and poached halibut. One day, I saw Chef Ripert happily drinking the daikon's braising liquid, and it struck me: That's where the flavor is, not in the daikon itself. It reminded me of pot likker (see Note), and I was immediately transported back to Georgia in my mind. Serve this as a Southerner would alongside a warm batch of cornbread to sop up all that flavorful pot likker—all the better if it's Lap Cheong Cornbread (page 120).

2 tablespoons canola oil

3 cloves garlic, thinly sliced

1-inch (2.5 cm) piece fresh ginger, sliced ¼ inch (6 mm) thick

3 ham hocks (about 9 ounces / 255 g each)

3 star anise pods

2 bay leaves

6 to 8 cilantro stems and ½ cup (8 g) cilantro leaves

12 ounces (340 g) daikon, roughly cut into 1-inch (2.5 cm) cubes (about 2½ cups)

1 teaspoon toasted sesame oil

¼ cup (60 ml) rice vinegar

Salt and black pepper

In a 5-quart (4.7 L) saucepan, heat the canola oil over medium heat. Add the garlic and ginger and cook, stirring occasionally, until they are lightly browned, about 2 minutes.

Carefully add 2½ quarts (2.4 L) water to the pot, then add the ham hocks, star anise, bay leaves, and cilantro stems and bring to a boil. Loosely cover the pot, reduce the heat to maintain a low simmer, and cook until the ham hocks are very tender, about 2½ hours. Add the daikon to the pot and cook, uncovered, until it is tender, 30 to 45 minutes longer.

Remove the ham hocks and let cool slightly, then remove all the meat from the bones. Discard the bones and add the meat back into the saucepan. Stir in the sesame oil and vinegar and season with salt and black pepper. Garnish with the cilantro leaves and serve right away.

NOTE:

Pot likker is a Southern staple, a delicious by-product once thought of as a throw-away food; in fact, as my friend John T. Edge wrote in his book *The Potlikker Papers*, pot likker was a food passed off to enslaved people in the Antebellum South. It usually results from braising hearty greens like collards with some sort of smoked pork product, oftentimes ham hocks. The liquor produced by this process is delicious, great for sopping up with cornbread or slurping on its own, and is actually sold as a side dish in Southern restaurants to those who know the flavor and nutrition lies in the liquid of pot likker, more so than the greens or pork.

Chinese Red-Cooked Pork Belly

SERVES 2 AS A MAIN COURSE

This rich pork belly preparation is a guilty pleasure of mine. Taking inspiration from the Chinese technique of tea smoking, where food is cooked over a smoking mixture of rice and tea leaves in a wok, I utilize Southern-style sweet tea (see Note) in the pork's braising liquid. Traditionally, the red hue of this dish comes from a combination of the pork, soy sauce, and sugar cane–derived rock sugar, but I swap in sorghum syrup for the latter, which gives the pork a darker amber color. Serve it with a side of Grilled Okra with Mala Oil (page 26) and ladle the sauce from the pork over some Lap Cheong Cornbread (page 120) or Fundamental Steamed Rice (page 87).

2 pounds (910 g) pork belly, cut into 1-inch (2.5 cm) cubes

2½ cups (600 ml) cold black tea

⅓ cup (75 ml) sorghum syrup

¼ cup (60 ml) soy sauce

3 star anise pods

1 stalk lemongrass, cut in half, top half discarded, bottom half split lengthwise and bruised with the side of a knife (optional)

In a medium pot, cover the pork belly with water and bring to a boil over high heat. When a boil is reached, remove from the heat and strain, discarding the water.

Add the tea, sorghum syrup, soy sauce, star anise, and lemongrass, if using, to the pot with the pork and bring to a boil over high heat. Reduce the heat to maintain a simmer and cook without a lid until the pork is tender, 1½ to 1¾ hours, skimming any scum that rises to the surface (the cooking liquid will reduce and thicken during this time).

Stir the pork to distribute the sauce and transfer to a serving bowl. Discard the lemongrass and drizzle any excess sauce over the pork. Serve immediately.

NOTE:

Southern sweet tea is simply iced black tea that has been sweetened with simple syrup based on personal preference. I like it "half and half" for drinking; we approximate that here with the sorghum syrup and plain, unsweetened black tea.

Bo Ssam Pulled Pork

SERVES 6 TO 8 AS A MAIN COURSE

Few dishes for large gatherings pack as much punch with so little stress as the classic Korean bo ssam. It's incredibly delicious, cost effective, impressive to behold on a table, and a fun way to get guests interacting at dinner parties in our home. Usually accompanied by banchan (several small dishes including various cooked and pickled vegetables), the fall-apart pork in this Chinese-influenced version pairs well with Fundamental Steamed Rice (page 87), Crushed Garlic and Cucumber Salad (page 39), Hoisin-Roasted Eggplant (page 44), Grilled Okra with Mala Oil (page 26), a bit of kimchi, and plenty of lettuce leaves to wrap it all up.

3 pounds (1.4 kg) boneless pork shoulder

FOR THE BRINE:

¼ cup (60 g) Chinese fermented black beans, rinsed

3 cloves garlic, crushed with the side of a chef's knife

2-inch (5 cm) piece fresh ginger, cut into ¼-inch (6 mm) pieces

4 star anise pods

1 tablespoon whole black peppercorns

1 tablespoon salt

¼ cup (60 ml) dark soy sauce

¼ cup (60 ml) apple cider vinegar

¾ cup (180 ml) sorghum syrup

1 quart (960 ml) ice water

FOR THE BASTE:

1 cup (240 ml) brine from above, strained

2 tablespoons hoisin sauce

2 tablespoons sorghum syrup

FOR THE SAUCE:

3 cups (720 ml) brine from above

1 tablespoon canola oil

5 green onions, green and white and parts, cut into 2-inch (5 cm) pieces

3 tablespoons gochujang

3 tablespoons hoisin sauce

2 tablespoons Mala Oil (page 247)

1 teaspoon toasted sesame oil

Salt and white pepper

Place the pork in a large, nonreactive container and set aside.

MAKE THE BRINE: In a medium saucepan, combine the black beans, garlic, ginger, star anise, peppercorns, salt, soy sauce, vinegar, sorghum syrup, and 1 quart (960 ml) water over high heat and bring to a boil. Stir until the salt is dissolved, then remove from the heat and add the ice water to cool the brine down. Pour the cooled brine over the pork, making sure it is fully submerged, cover, and refrigerate for at least 4 hours or up to overnight.

When ready to proceed, preheat the oven to 350°F (175°C) and line a baking sheet with parchment paper. Remove the pork from the brine, shaking the pork to remove excess liquid, and place the pork onto the baking sheet. Set aside.

Strain the brine through a sieve, discarding the solids and reserving 5 cups (1.2 L) of brine.

MAKE THE BASTE: In a medium bowl, whisk 2 cups (480 ml) of the reserved brine, the hoisin sauce, and sorghum syrup to combine.

Tightly cover the pork with aluminum foil, place in the oven, and roast, brushing the pork with the baste every 20 minutes, re-covering with foil each time, until the pork is deeply lacquered and fall-apart tender with an internal temperature between 190 and 200°F (87 and 90°C), about 3½ hours.

MEANWHILE, MAKE THE SAUCE: In a small saucepan, bring 3 cups (720 ml) of the reserved brine to a simmer over high heat and reduce the brine to roughly ½ cup (120 ml). Remove from the heat and set aside. In a large sauté pan, heat the canola oil over high heat. When thin wisps of smoke rise from the pan, add the green onions to the pan and lightly brown, stirring once, about 15 seconds. Remove the green onions from the pan and let cool slightly. Chop the green onions into small pieces and place in a small bowl. Add the gochujang, hoisin sauce, mala oil, and sesame oil, and season with salt and white pepper. Add the reduced brine and whisk together. Set aside.

When the pork is done, let rest for 30 minutes, then transfer to a large serving platter, with a couple of large serving forks for shredding the pork, along with the sauce and desired accompaniments.

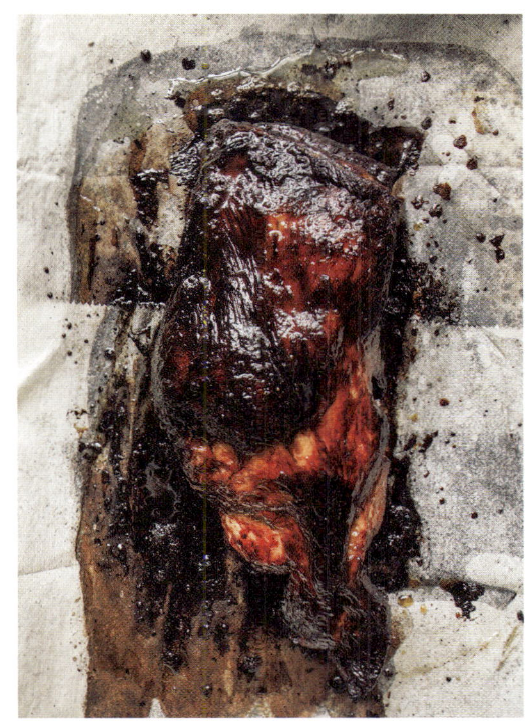

Fried Pork Chops with Sweet and Sour Sauce

SERVES 4 AS A MAIN COURSE

Pork chops have always been a favorite of mine, breaded and fried in traditional Southern style, maybe smothered with pan drippings, perhaps some tangy applesauce on the side. But I also ate a lot of the classic, saucy Peking-style chops at big, banquet-style Chinese dinners. This dish is a natural progression from my early love of both styles of sweet, sour, saucy chops, especially with a bowl of Fundamental Steamed Rice (page 87) and a side of Stir-Fried Collard Greens with Bacon (page 51).

4 boneless pork loin chops (8 ounces / 225 g each), trimmed

2 large eggs, beaten

2 cups plus 1 teaspoon (255 g plus 3 g) cornstarch

1 tablespoon Chinese five-spice powder

1 tablespoon salt

½ teaspoon ground white pepper

¼ cup (60 ml) plus 1 tablespoon canola oil

1 tablespoon soy sauce

2½ tablespoons Worcestershire sauce

1 teaspoon toasted sesame oil

3 cloves garlic, thinly sliced

1-inch (2.5 cm) piece peeled fresh ginger, cut into 1 by ¼-inch (2.5 cm by 6 mm) matchstick strips

¼ cup (60 ml) ketchup

1 tablespoon oyster sauce

2 tablespoons sorghum syrup

½ cup (120 ml) Chicken Stock (page 189)

1 tablespoon toasted sesame seeds

1 tablespoon sliced green onion (1 medium), green part only

With a meat mallet, or between two sheets of plastic wrap or waxed paper with a rolling pin, pound the pork chops to ¼-inch (6 mm) thickness. Cut into rough 2½-inch (6 cm) squares and set aside.

Place the beaten eggs in a wide, shallow dish. Place the 2 cups (255 g) cornstarch, Chinese five-spice powder, salt, and white pepper in another wide, shallow dish and mix well. Place 1 piece of pork chop in the eggs and flip the chop so both sides are covered with egg. Gently shake the excess egg from the pork, then place the pork in the seasoned cornstarch and coat with the mixture, firmly pressing so the mixture adheres. Repeat with all of the pork and set aside.

In a large skillet, heat ¼ cup (60 ml) of the canola oil over medium-high heat. Add the pork, in batches if necessary, and cook until it is well browned, about 3 minutes on each side, using a slotted spoon to transfer the browned pork to a bowl. When all the pork has been browned, remove the pan from the heat, wipe it clean with paper towels, and set aside.

Combine the soy sauce, Worcestershire sauce, sesame oil, the remaining 1 teaspoon (3 g) cornstarch, and 2 tablespoons water in a small bowl and whisk to make a slurry. Set aside.

Return the skillet to medium heat and add the remaining 1 tablespoon canola oil. Add the garlic and ginger and stir constantly to infuse them into the oil until they are lightly browned, about 15 seconds. Add the ketchup, oyster sauce, and sorghum syrup and stir constantly for 10 seconds to avoid burning. Add the stock, stir well, and bring the mixture to a boil. Whisk the slurry once more, then add to the sauce while whisking and allow the sauce to come back up to a boil. Add the chops and stir well to completely coat them in the sauce.

Transfer to a serving platter and sprinkle with the sesame seeds and green onion. Serve immediately.

Lemongrass Pork Chops

SERVES 4 AS A MAIN COURSE

In Vietnamese restaurants, I always gravitate to the marinated and grilled meat section of the menu. This marinade, aromatic with lemongrass and ginger, works especially well with pork chops but would be delicious with chicken or salmon as well. Once the meat is caramelized and smoky from the grill, this dish is hard to beat. Plus, it's pretty versatile. Slice the pork thinly and slide it into a baguette with some cucumbers, carrots, and cilantro for a quick banh mi sandwich, or serve the chops as part of a larger spread with fragrant Fundamental Steamed Rice (page 87) or Vietnamese bun rice noodles, Grilled Okra with Mala Oil (page 26), and Asian Pear and Napa Cabbage Slaw (page 52). Or just place them atop some buttery mashed potatoes for a Vietnamese take on American comfort food.

FOR THE MARINADE:

2 stalks lemongrass, top half removed and discarded, bottom half cut crosswise into thin slices

2 cloves garlic

1-inch (2.5 cm) piece fresh ginger, cut into ¼-inch (6 mm) pieces

2 green onions, green and white parts, thinly sliced

½ teaspoon ground white pepper

1 tablespoon fish sauce

2 tablespoons sorghum syrup

1 teaspoon toasted sesame oil

1 tablespoon whiskey

1 tablespoon canola oil

4 (6-ounce / 170 g) boneless pork loin chops, gently pounded with a meat mallet to ⅓-inch (8 mm) thickness

Salt

MAKE THE MARINADE: Place the lemongrass, garlic, ginger, green onions, white pepper, fish sauce, sorghum syrup, sesame oil, whiskey, and canola oil in a food processor and pulse to a loose, chunky consistency rather than a smooth, homogenous one.

Place the pork chops and roughly ¼ cup (60 ml) of the marinade in a zip-top plastic bag. Massage the pork chops to distribute the marinade and refrigerate for at least 4 hours or up to overnight.

Remove the pork chops from the refrigerator roughly 1 hour before cooking. Preheat your clean and seasoned grill (see Note, page 159) over medium heat. Season the pork chops with salt, place them on the hot grill, and do not move them for 4 minutes.

Flip the pork chops and finish cooking through, until a meat thermometer inserted in the thickest part of the meat reaches 145°F (63°C), another 3 to 4 minutes. Serve immediately.

Pork, Daikon, and Collard Green Adobo

SERVES 4 TO 6 AS A MAIN COURSE

Adobo is a widespread dish in the Philippines, so commonplace that it can even be referred to as a technique wherein a main ingredient (usually but not necessarily meat) is slowly cooked with a fair amount of vinegar, resulting in a deliciously tangy and tender final product. My version is still a simple braise with a high payoff, but I also like to incorporate hearty collard greens and crunchy daikon, and while adobo is great with steamed jasmine rice, it's just as tasty ladled over hot grits, Collard Green Fried Rice (page 73), or even on a crumbled slice of Lap Cheong Cornbread (page 120). This is pure, comforting Asian soul food, a dish I've made many times for friends and family as part of a care package that always hits the spot.

2 pounds (910 g) boneless pork shoulder blade roast (fresh pork butt), cut into 1-inch (2.5 cm) cubes

Salt and black pepper

2 tablespoons canola oil

8 cloves garlic, crushed with the side of a chef's knife

1-inch (2.5 cm) piece fresh ginger, cut into ¼-inch (6 mm) pieces

3 shallots, peeled and quartered

1½ teaspoons coarsely ground black pepper

1½ cups (360 ml) rice vinegar

1½ cups (360 ml) Chicken Stock (page 189) or water

2 bay leaves

3 star anise pods

1 teaspoon soy sauce

1 teaspoon fish sauce

10 ounces (280 g) daikon, cut into 1-inch (2.5 cm) cubes (about 2 cups)

4 ounces (115 g) collard greens, cleaned and chopped (1 cup loosely packed)

4½ teaspoons brown sugar

Season the pork with salt and black pepper and set aside.

In a 5-quart (4.7 L) Dutch oven, heat 1 tablespoon of the oil over medium-high heat. When thin wisps of smoke form, add half of the pork and cook until browned all over, 1 to 2 minutes per side, using a slotted spoon to transfer the meat to a bowl after it is browned. Repeat with the remaining oil and remaining pork.

When all of the pork is browned, remove all but roughly 1 tablespoon of the fat remaining in the pot and reduce the heat to low. Add the garlic, ginger, and shallots to the pot and cook, stirring occasionally, until the vegetables begin to brown, about 2 minutes. Add the coarsely ground black pepper to the pot and cook for 1 to 2 minutes to infuse it into the other ingredients. Add the vinegar, stock, bay leaves, star anise, soy sauce, and fish sauce to the pot and stir well. Nestle the pork back into the pot, adjust the heat to maintain a simmer, and cover the pot loosely to prevent too much reduction. Simmer until the pork is tender, about 2 hours, then add the daikon, loosely cover, and simmer for another 15 minutes. Add the collard greens and cook until tender, about 5 minutes longer.

Stir in the brown sugar, adjust the seasoning, and serve immediately. Refrigerate leftovers and all liquids in an airtight container for up to 1 week.

Chinese Pork Jerky

SERVES 4 TO 6 AS A SNACK

Commonly known as *bak kwa*, this salty, slightly sweet Chinese treat is a quick and tasty snack on its own, or a flavorful ingredient sliced into thin strips for noodle salads. It's a great addition to a banh mi or used as a substitute for bacon in a classic BLT, or left in larger sheets and stacked with cucumbers, scrambled eggs, and chile sauce for a Malaysian-style sandwich. I like to buy a piece of pork butt and grind it myself, throwing the bacon in the grinder as well, but feel free to simply buy ground pork and finely chop the bacon by hand.

FOR THE JERKY:

1 pound (455 g) ground pork

4 ounces (115 g) ground bacon (or finely chopped)

1 tablespoon sorghum syrup

1 tablespoon hoisin sauce

1½ teaspoons Chinese five-spice powder

1 teaspoon fish sauce

3 dashes Tabasco sauce

½ teaspoon garlic powder

½ teaspoon ginger powder

½ teaspoon onion powder

Canola oil

FOR THE LACQUER:

¼ cup (60 ml) sorghum syrup

¼ cup (60 ml) hoisin sauce

MAKE THE JERKY: In a medium bowl, mix the pork, bacon, sorghum syrup, hoisin sauce, Chinese five-spice powder, fish sauce, Tabasco, garlic powder, ginger powder, and onion powder well by hand or with a wooden spoon. Cover and refrigerate until chilled through, 30 to 60 minutes.

When ready to proceed, preheat the oven to 400°F (205°C) and grease two 18 by 26-inch (46 by 66 cm) sheets of parchment paper with canola oil. Place the chilled meat mixture on the greased side of one sheet of parchment paper and spread it into a thin layer using a rubber spatula. Place the other sheet of parchment paper greased-side down on top of the meat.

Using a rolling pin, press the meat into an even layer roughly 1/16 inch (2 mm) thick. Carefully peel off the top layer of parchment paper, keeping the meat in one layer (if some meat sticks to the top sheet of paper, use the spatula to fill any gaps). Transfer the meat, still on the bottom sheet of parchment paper, to a baking sheet, then place into the preheated oven. Roast until cooked through, about 6 minutes.

WHILE THE PORK IS COOKING, MAKE THE LACQUER: Combine the sorghum syrup and hoisin sauce in a small bowl and mix to combine. When the pork is done, remove it from the oven and adjust the oven control to a high broil. Using a spatula, carefully transfer the meat from the parchment paper to a wire rack, then transfer the rack to the baking sheet. Brush the top of the meat with the lacquer, then broil until the lacquer starts to bubble and caramelize a bit without burning, about 2 minutes. Remove the tray from the oven, carefully flip the meat, and brush again with the lacquer. Return to the broiler and cook again until the lacquer is bubbling and caramelized, but not burnt, 2 to 3 minutes. Remove from the oven and allow to fully cool, about 15 to 20 minutes. Cut into rough 2-inch (5 cm) squares and store in an airtight container in the refrigerator for up to 1 week.

Char Siu Glazed Baby Back Ribs

SERVES 4 AS A MAIN COURSE

Southern-style barbecued pork ribs were one of my favorite dishes growing up. To me they have as strong a Southern identity as collard greens or their pot likker, probably because I ate them so much. These particular ribs were developed in an effort to win brownie points with my mother-in-law, Julie, who used to bring this dish to potluck picnics when my wife, Jackie, was growing up in Connecticut. If you want to get on the good side of your friends and family, I suggest you incorporate these ribs into your repertoire as well! Here, I've adapted her honey-garlic-soy sauce ribs to this version over a couple dozen attempts to build a fitting tribute without copying her recipe directly.

These ribs have a very Chinese flavor profile from the Char Siu Marinade (page 244), but we also keep it sweet and Southern with the addition of sorghum syrup. Into smoked meats? Well, we wrote this recipe for a home oven, but if you want to really elevate these ribs with a smoky Southern spin, cook them low and slow and off to the side over a wood fire, which is my preferred method anytime I get the chance to do so.

½ cup (120 ml) Char Siu Marinade (page 244)

2 racks pork baby back ribs (1 pound / 455 g each), silver skin removed from underside

Salt and white pepper

FOR THE BASTE:

½ cup (120 ml) Char Siu Marinade (page 244)

1 tablespoon apple cider vinegar

FOR THE LACQUER:

¼ cup (60 ml) Char Siu Marinade (page 244)

2 tablespoons sorghum syrup

2 tablespoons hoisin sauce

3 green onions, green parts sliced on the bias, white parts left whole and used as a brush (see Note, page 200)

Rub ½ cup (120 ml) char siu marinade on both sides of the ribs. Cover and refrigerate for at least 4 hours or up to overnight to marinate. Remove the ribs from the refrigerator about 1 hour before you are ready to cook and season with salt and white pepper.

Preheat the oven to 350°F (175°C).

In a small bowl, make the baste by combining ½ cup (120 ml) char siu marinade with the vinegar; mix well. Line a baking sheet with foil and place a roasting rack large enough to hold the 2 racks of ribs on the foil-lined baking sheet. Place the ribs on the rack bone side up and place in the preheated oven. Cook the ribs, brushing the bone side with the baste every 15 minutes. After the ribs have cooked for 1 hour and 15 minutes, remove them from the oven and flip them so the meat side is up. Return to the oven for another 1 hour and 15 minutes, basting the meat side every 15 minutes.

Meanwhile, in a small bowl, make the lacquer by combining the ¼ cup (60 ml) char siu marinade with the sorghum syrup and hoisin sauce; mix well.

After the ribs have cooked for a total of 2½ hours (see Note), remove them from the oven, adjust the oven control to broil, and generously brush the meat side of the ribs with all of the lacquer.

When the broiler is preheated, return the ribs to the oven and allow the lacquer to bubble and caramelize for 3 to 4 minutes, being careful not to burn it.

Remove the ribs from the oven, let them cool slightly, then cut the ribs into individual bones. Place the bones on a serving platter, sprinkle with green onions, and serve immediately.

NOTE:

If you prefer "fall off the bone ribs," cook for 3½ hours before broiling; if you like a bit more chew, only cook for about 2 hours before broiling. I personally like that Goldilocks *just right* balance between chew and tenderness at the 2½ hours listed in the recipe.

Char Siu Pulled Pork

SERVES 6 TO 8 AS A MAIN COURSE

Pork and barbecue sauce go together like peas and carrots, so it was a forgone conclusion to combine pulled pork with the tangy sweetness of my Char Siu Marinade (see page 244)—the thick, umami-rich sauce creates a wonderful lacquer. Using a smoker will produce incredible results, but we've written this recipe for an oven so everyone can get in on the tasty fun. Pull the pork with a couple of forks and serve it with steamed rice, kimchi, and Bibb lettuce for wraps, or pile it into a bun with store-bought Vietnamese and bread and butter pickles and Asian Pear and Napa Cabbage Slaw (page 52) to make Southern-style sandwiches.

FOR THE BRINE:

1 cup (240 ml) Char Siu Marinade (page 244)

2 quarts (2 L) cold water

¼ cup (60 ml) apple cider vinegar

¼ cup (60 ml) dark soy sauce

2 tablespoons Chinese five-spice powder

3 cloves garlic, crushed with the side of a chef's knife

2-inch (5 cm) piece fresh ginger, cut crosswise into ¼-inch (6 mm) slices

3 pounds (1.4 kg) boneless pork shoulder

FOR THE BASTE:

1 cup (240 ml) Char Siu Marinade (page 244)

MAKE THE BRINE: Combine all of the brine ingredients in a nonreactive container large enough to hold the pork and mix well. Remove ½ cup (120 ml) of the brine and reserve. Add the pork to the brine, cover, and refrigerate for at least 4 hours or up to overnight.

When ready to proceed, preheat oven to 300°F (150°C). Line a baking sheet with parchment paper and place a wire rack on the pan.

MAKE THE BASTE: In a small bowl, combine the reserved brine with the char siu marinade and mix well. Remove the pork from the brine and discard the used brine. Place the pork on the wire rack. Brush the baste all over the pork and place the pork into the oven. Cook the pork until fork tender, about 5 hours, basting it every 30 minutes (if the pork seems like it is getting too dark too fast and threatens to burn, cover it with aluminum foil).

Remove the pork from the oven and allow it to rest for 30 minutes, then shred the pork with forks or a knife and serve immediately.

Vietnamese-Style Caramel Pork Belly

SERVES 4 AS A MAIN COURSE

Everyone loves bacon, but this pork belly, popular in Vietnam, is my favorite way to eat the part of the pig that bacon comes from. It's decadent and comforting, with a beautiful dark amber glaze from the sorghum syrup. Serve this sticky and sweet pork over grits or Fundamental Steamed Rice (page 87) with braised collard greens, or even Collard Green Fried Rice (page 73).

3 pounds (1.4 kg) pork belly, cut into ½-inch (12 mm) cubes

⅓ cup (75 g) packed light brown sugar

2 stalks lemongrass, top half removed and discarded, bottom half halved crosswise and crushed with the side of a chef's knife

1-inch (2.5 cm) piece fresh ginger, peeled and cut into ¼-inch (6 mm) pieces

2 makrut lime leaves

½ cup (120 ml) sorghum syrup

3 tablespoons fish sauce

Place the pork belly in a medium saucepan, cover with water, and set over high heat. When the water comes to a boil, drain the water and set the pork aside.

Clean and dry the same pot and add the sugar to it. Place over medium-low heat and cook, swirling the pan occasionally, until the sugar is caramelized to a deep amber color, 8 to 9 minutes. Using caution against sizzling and spitting, carefully add 3 cups (720 ml) water to the caramel.

Stir and bring to a boil, then reduce the heat to maintain a simmer and add the lemongrass, ginger, lime leaves, sorghum syrup, fish sauce, and pork and slowly simmer until the pork is tender and the sauce has reduced to a glaze, 45 to 60 minutes. Serve immediately.

NOTE:

In principle, caramel is simple to make, but proper steps should be taken to do so, as should care and caution while working with the extremely high temperatures produced. You are gradually altering the structure of sugar, so let the process happen gradually and don't be tempted to crank the heat. Swirl the pan gently as needed so as to leave the sugar as one unit, rather than up the sides of the pan. If you do stir, be careful where you lay the spoon, as it will have super-hot sugar on it, plus you don't want to introduce foreign substances to the caramel the next time you stir, which could cause crystallization of the caramel. Finally, when you pour the water into the caramel in this recipe, it will cause a strong reaction, so stay calm and pour slowly and carefully, swirling and/or stirring until the caramel has dissolved into the water.

Chinese Sausage and Fresh Field Peas Salad

SERVES 2 AS A MAIN COURSE OR 4 TO 6 AS A SIDE

Technically, most varieties of field peas are actually beans, but that sort of semantic doesn't matter when you're enjoying these Southern beauties—the most well-known of which is the black-eyed pea—found in farmers' markets at the height of the Georgia summer. Originally brought from West Africa to the United States by enslaved people, they are grown by farmers to balance nitrogen levels in their fields. If you're lucky enough, you can explore heirloom varieties such as Whippoorwill, Dimpled Brown Crowder, and Turkey Craw. If not, canned beans work great in this salad loaded with herbs, salty Chinese sausage, and a bright dressing.

Salt

1 pound (455 g) fresh field peas, about 3 cups (see Note)

3 links (1½ ounces / 43 g each) lap cheong (Chinese sausage, see page 18), quartered lengthwise and sliced ¼ inch (6 mm) thick

FOR THE VINAIGRETTE:

1 tablespoon honey

1 tablespoon rice vinegar

2 tablespoons olive oil

1½ teaspoons fish sauce

Juice of ½ lime (about 1 tablespoon)

½ teaspoon minced ginger

¼ cup (40 g) roasted peanuts

¼ cup (4 g) cilantro leaves

¼ cup (4 g) basil leaves

¼ cup (4 g) mint leaves

½ small Honeycrisp apple, peeled, cored, and cut into ¼-inch (6 mm) cubes, about ¼ cup (30 g)

1½ teaspoons minced shallot

½ medium carrot, peeled and diced into ¼-inch (6 mm) pieces, about ¼ cup (30 g)

Salt and white pepper

Fill a medium pot with water, add a heavy pinch of salt, and bring to a boil over high heat. Add the field peas and cook for 3½ minutes, or until they are tender and soft. Add the lap cheong and cook for an additional 15 seconds, then strain through a colander, discarding the water and rinsing the peas and sausage under cold water until cool. Set aside to drain thoroughly.

MAKE THE VINAIGRETTE: In a medium bowl, combine the honey, vinegar, olive oil, fish sauce, lime juice, and ginger and whisk until thoroughly combined.

When the peas and sausage are thoroughly drained, place them in a large bowl and add the peanuts, cilantro, basil, mint, apple, shallot, and carrot and season with salt and white pepper. Add all of the vinaigrette, gently toss together, then serve immediately. Leftovers can be refrigerated for up to 1 week.

NOTE:

If you can't find fresh field peas, canned chickpeas or black-eyed peas will work; just skip boiling them. Simply give the peas a rinse and drain well. You will still need to blanch the sausage for 15 seconds as directed.

Smoked Ham Hock and Seaweed Soup

SERVES 4 TO 6 AS A MAIN COURSE

My mom's pork neck and seaweed soup was a family favorite growing up, and it helped me understand the beauty and value of the parts of the pig beyond the succulent chops and slow-roasted shoulders. Her version was pure and simple: Put raw ingredients in a pot, add water, and simmer all day, filling the house with rich aromas from the soup that we'd enjoy that evening, eating bowl after bowl. My version also incorporates inspiration from the Japanese master stock dashi, using umami-rich kombu as well as smoky ham hocks in place of the smoked bonito known as *katsuobushi*, bringing a savory depth and complexity to the soup before removing the kombu and bones. Any meat is picked from the bones and returned to the soup before finishing it with the wakame, plus a little egg drop in a nod to my Chinese ancestry. I like this soup best next to a bowl of Fundamental Steamed Rice (page 87).

2 tablespoons canola oil

2 cups (320 g) chopped onion

8 cloves garlic, thinly sliced

4-inch (10 cm) piece fresh ginger, sliced ¼ inch (6 mm) thick

4 pounds (1.8 kg) ham hocks (about 8 to 12 hocks)

4 pieces kombu, each roughly 8 by 4 inches (20 by 10 cm) (see Note)

2 tablespoons dried wakame seaweed (see Note)

1 tablespoon toasted sesame oil

4 large eggs, beaten

In a 5-quart (4.7 L) saucepan, heat the canola oil over medium heat. Add the onion, garlic, and ginger and cook, stirring occasionally, until the onions have softened, about 2 minutes. Add 5 quarts (4.7 L) water and the ham hocks to the pot and bring to a simmer. Add the kombu, reduce the heat to maintain a simmer, and cook for 3 hours to develop a flavorful stock, replenishing the water to maintain the original level as needed.

Remove the pot from the heat and remove the kombu and ham hocks, discarding the kombu. When cool enough to handle, pull the meat off the ham hocks, discard the bones and inedible cartilage, and return about 8 ounces (225 g) meat to the pot, more or less as desired, and save the remaining meat for another use. Add the wakame seaweed to the pot and place over medium heat.

When the liquid begins to simmer, stir in the sesame oil and slowly drizzle the eggs into the pot while stirring. Let cook for about 20 seconds, until the eggs form cooked strands, then remove the pot from the heat and serve immediately. Refrigerate leftovers in an airtight container for up to 1 week.

NOTE:

Look for both the thick kelp known as *kombu* as well as wakame seaweed in Asian markets or online. Keep an eye out for the white, salt-like substance running up and down the sheets of kombu—that's the protein-rich glutamic acid that delivers kombu's umami punch. Wakame seaweed, often rehydrated for use in seaweed salads, will rehydrate in the soup and bring a briny flavor and snappy texture.

Lap Cheong Cornbread

SERVES 4 TO 6 AS A SIDE

For something so widely loved, cornbread can be a bit divisive. There are those who scoff at the sweetened kind, and those who won't want the salty type. I grew up with a fairly sweet rendition, until my mother discovered Harold's Barbecue about a half hour south of the Atlanta airport. Their cast-iron skillet version was caramelized and crispy on the bottom, with crispy bits of pork crackling floating around, and the only sweetness coming from the corn itself. We never looked back. This version swaps in Chinese lap cheong for the salty pork cracklings, its savoriness amplified by the bits of browned green onions. Smooth it all out by serving it with a bit of butter or a dollop of sour cream.

3 teaspoons canola oil

3 links (1½ ounces / 43 g each) lap cheong (Chinese sausage, see page 18), quartered lengthwise and sliced ¼ inch (6 mm) thick

6 green onions, white and green parts, cut into ¼-inch (6 mm) pieces

2 cups (300 g) self-rising medium grind cornmeal (see Notes)

1 teaspoon salt

2¼ cups (540 ml) full-fat buttermilk

2 large eggs

8 tablespoons (110 g) unsalted butter, melted and slightly cooled

Preheat the oven to 425°F (220°C).

In a well-seasoned 9-inch (23 cm) cast-iron pan (see Notes), heat 2 teaspoons of the oil over medium heat. Add the lap cheong and green onions and cook, stirring occasionally, until lightly browned, 5 to 6 minutes. Transfer the lap cheong and green onions to a small bowl and allow to cool for 10 minutes. Wipe the pan clean with a paper towel and set aside.

In a large bowl, combine the cornmeal and salt and mix well. In another bowl, whisk the buttermilk and eggs until smooth. Whisk in the melted butter (it will quickly solidify into small chunks; this is OK), then add this mixture to the cornmeal and stir until combined. Add the reserved lap cheong and green onions to the batter and stir just until incorporated.

Place the pan over medium-low heat and heat for 2 minutes. Add the remaining 1 teaspoon oil and swirl to coat the pan. Pour the batter into the pan (it should sizzle), shake and tap the pan to make sure the batter is level, then place in the preheated oven.

Bake until a toothpick inserted in the center comes out clean, 20 to 30 minutes, then remove the cornbread from oven and let it cool slightly before serving in the skillet.

NOTES:

Self-rising cornmeal is a staple in the South, simply a cornmeal with a bit of a leavening agent and salt mixed in. If you'd rather make your own for this recipe, mix 2 cups (300 g) medium grind cornmeal, 1 tablespoon baking powder, and 1 teaspoon salt together and substitute for the 2 cups (300 g) self-rising cornmeal.

To season a cast-iron pan, place 3 tablespoons kosher salt in the pan and place it over medium heat for 15 minutes. Reduce the heat to low and use a dry paper towel to carefully scrub the salt into the pan, aiming to remove any sediment, for about 2 minutes. Pour the hot salt into your sink (avoid the trash can so you don't melt the plastic bag), then pour 1 tablespoon canola oil into the hot pan, still over low heat. Coat the inside of the pan (including the sides) with the oil using a paper towel. The oil will help remove any sediment as it penetrates the iron, seasoning it. Remove from the heat; the pan is now seasoned.

CHAPTER 4

Seafood

Buford Highway

"Dirty South" is a name given to hip-hop music from the South by rappers in the nineties in an effort to gain respect and recognition at a time when the art form was mainly portrayed as an East Coast or West Coast thing. It's a term that embraces the good and the bad of the South's historical identity; it's a badge that everyone from the South can wear with pride.

To me, it can also be applied to food. Much in the same way the Southern rappers wanted to be acknowledged despite being new and different from the norm, we're producing food in the South that's distinct to what's happening in other American regions, and in my heart, this food identity is an important aspect of the term *Dirty South*.

The epitome of *my* Dirty South is Atlanta's Buford Highway. It's a "dirty" hodgepodge of Southern, Asian, and Hispanic cultures, full of restaurants and markets where I can still learn

about food to this day. The Buford Highway Farmers Market is loaded with fresh tortillas to chicharrons, pierogis to pork bao. P N Rice Cake House sells my favorite kimchi, made by a Korean grandmother named Grace Yu on site. A restaurant called Mamak serves some of the best Malaysian food this side of Melaka and Best BBQ has dim sum and Cantonese-style roasted meats that always hit the spot. Plus, this is where I had Chinese lessons as a kid before getting big steaming bowls of Vietnamese pho!

My food—from Lazy Betty to this book—takes inspiration ranging from places as different as the American South to my culinary school experience in Australia to the three Michelin-starred Le Bernardin. But most importantly, it reflects this rich collection of cultures in this place we know as the South, and a flip through these pages is like a slow cruise down Buford Highway, full of the sights and sounds of the cultures who have made the South home, and who inspire me every day.

OPPOSITE: Ron shopping for condiments at a grocery store off Buford Highway.

ABOVE, LEFT: Ron at PN Rice Cakes with owner Grace Yu. ABOVE, RIGHT: Ron in China Town's food court, which is right outside where he went to Chinese school.

Shrimp with Chinese Soft Scrambled Eggs

SERVES 2 AS A MAIN COURSE

This Cantonese-inspired dish became a big hit in my household once I became a father. It's simple, quick, and I don't have to pull my daughter Calliope's teeth to eat it. The secret is to beat the eggs right before cooking to aerate them, making the eggs light and fluffy. While my French cooking background screams at me to not cook eggs over high heat, here it makes the eggs soufflé as the water and wine within them transforms into steam, producing a tender, fluffy finished product. Serve over Fundamental Steamed Rice (page 87) or grits for breakfast, for a spin on the classic Southern shrimp and grits.

12 ounces (340 g) shrimp, any size, shelled and deveined (about 1½ cups), preferably Royal Red (see Note)

1 teaspoon cornstarch

Salt and white pepper

4 large eggs

1 tablespoon Shaoxing cooking wine

½ teaspoon toasted sesame oil

3 tablespoons canola oil

1 green onion, green part only, thinly sliced

In a medium bowl, thoroughly combine the shrimp, cornstarch, and salt and white pepper to taste, then set aside.

In a small bowl, crack the eggs and whisk with the wine, sesame oil, and salt and white pepper to taste, then set aside.

Heat 2 tablespoons of the canola oil in a wok or large skillet over high heat, then add the shrimp and cook, stirring frequently, just until cooked through, 1 to 2 minutes.

Remove the shrimp, then add the remaining 1 tablespoon canola oil to the pan. Beat the eggs once more for about 10 seconds to aerate them, then add them to the pan and cook, letting a thin layer of cooked egg form, 10 to 20 seconds. Add the shrimp to the pan on top of the eggs, then gently fold the eggs and shrimp to create layers, being careful not to break the eggs up too much (the goal is to create multiple layers rather than a single layer of egg to encase the shrimp as you would if you were making a typical Western omelet). Take care not to overcook the eggs, only cooking them for about 20 to 30 seconds total.

Transfer to a plate, top with the green onions, and serve immediately.

NOTE:

I personally love Royal Red shrimp, wild-caught in the Gulf of Mexico. They turn from pale to vibrant pink when cooked, with a slightly sweet flavor and incredibly tender and delicate texture. However, any shrimp available to you will work well for this recipe.

Spicy Dry-Fried Catfish with Cilantro and Cumin

SERVES 2 AS A MAIN COURSE

True Southerners love catfish fried with a cornmeal crust and tartar sauce, but here, we move in a Szechuan direction, using a cornstarch dredge (dry-frying indicates that no batter is used), plenty of aromatics, and the numbing, spicy sensation of Mala Oil (page 247). Bump up the ingredients for a family-style spread with a cooling Mandarin Beef and Papaya Salad with Roasted Peanuts (page 160) and Fundamental Steamed Rice (page 87), tuck the fish into a baguette to make a spicy catfish po'boy, or simply drizzle it with Mala Oil.

1 pound (455 g) catfish fillets, cut into 2 by 1-inch (5 cm by 2.5 cm) pieces

1 tablespoon Shaoxing cooking wine

1 tablespoon soy sauce

½ teaspoon toasted sesame oil

⅔ cup (80 g) cornstarch

1 tablespoon ground cumin

1 tablespoon canola oil, plus more for deep-frying

2 cloves garlic, finely minced

1 tablespoon minced ginger

2 green onions, green and white parts, cut into ½-inch (12 mm) pieces

1½ teaspoons doubanjiang (see Note)

1 tablespoon Mala Oil (page 247)

¼ cup (4 g) cilantro leaves

Salt

In a medium bowl, gently mix the catfish, wine, soy sauce, and sesame oil. Allow to marinate, covered and refrigerated, for at least 10 minutes and up to 2 hours.

When ready to proceed, remove the fish from the marinade, gently shaking off any excess liquid, and place in a clean bowl. In a small bowl, combine the cornstarch and cumin and mix until combined. Sprinkle the cornstarch mixture over the fish and gently mix to evenly coat the fish, discarding any excess cornstarch, and set aside.

Set up a frying station. In a large, heavy pot set up with an oil thermometer, heat 2 inches (5 cm) canola oil over high heat to 350°F (175°C). Have a spider and paper towel–lined plate ready.

Working in batches as necessary to avoid overcrowding and dropping the oil temperature, gently lay the fish into the oil. Fry until golden brown, about 3 minutes, then use a spider to remove the fish from the oil, shaking off excess oil, and set on the paper towel–lined plate. Season the fish with salt.

Working quickly to prevent the catfish from getting soggy, heat the 1 tablespoon canola oil in a large skillet over medium heat. Add the garlic and ginger and stir constantly (stir-frying) to infuse them into the oil until they are lightly browned, about 10 seconds, taking care not to burn them. Add the green onions and stir-fry for another 30 seconds. Add the doubanjiang and stir-fry for another 30 seconds. Add the mala oil and stir-fry for another 30 seconds. Add the fish and cilantro and gently toss for 10 seconds to combine the ingredients, then transfer to a bowl and serve immediately.

NOTE:

Doubanjiang is a spicy fermented bean paste elemental to Szechuan cooking, found in Asian stores or online.

Grilled Salmon with Hoisin Barbecue Sauce

SERVES 2 AS A MAIN COURSE

As a young chef just out of culinary school, I used salmon in one of the first dishes I created back home in my mother's restaurant. It was a salmon croquette with pineapple relish, and it was delicious. But I really appreciate the straightforward beauty of simply grilling salmon. It's easier, far purer, and even better than that croquette in the early days. Better still, my daughter Calliope who loves salmon can't resist this preparation of her favorite food, lured in by the sweetness of the hoisin barbecue sauce. Pair it with Grilled Okra with Mala Oil (page 26), Crushed Garlic and Cucumber Salad (page 39), kimchi, and Fundamental Steamed Rice (page 87), or even a Southern potato salad, and you've got a fun cookout going.

FOR THE SAUCE:

½ cup (120 ml) hoisin sauce

½ teaspoon minced, peeled fresh ginger

1 clove garlic, minced

1 tablespoon apple cider vinegar

1 tablespoon Worcestershire sauce

1 tablespoon ketchup

1 teaspoon light soy sauce

¼ cup (60 ml) cold, unsweetened black tea

2 pieces salmon fillet (4 to 6 ounces / 115 to 170 g each), skin and pinbones removed

1 tablespoon canola oil

Salt and white pepper

MAKE THE SAUCE: In a small bowl, combine the hoisin sauce, ginger, garlic, vinegar, Worcestershire sauce, ketchup, soy sauce, and tea and whisk to combine. Reserve ¼ cup (60 ml) of the marinade and brush enough of the remaining marinade on the salmon to coat it (any excess marinade can be frozen for later use) and refrigerate, uncovered, for at least 30 minutes or up to 2 hours to marinate. Remove the salmon from the refrigerator roughly 30 minutes before you are ready to proceed.

Preheat your clean and seasoned grill over medium heat.

Gently remove any excess marinade from the fish with a paper towel, then rub the fish with canola oil and season it with salt and white pepper to taste. Place the salmon on the hot grill, top side down, and do not move it for 30 to 60 seconds (see Note) to allow it to get nice grill marks. Rotate the fish 45 degrees and cook for another 30 to 60 seconds to get crosshatch marks. Flip the fish and repeat the previous process, brushing the top side with reserved marinade.

Transfer the fish to serving plates and brush with the reserved marinade once and serve immediately.

NOTE:

The cook time for a medium-rare piece of fish (my preferred doneness for a juicy middle) is 2 to 3 minutes per side; adjust depending on your preference and the heat of your grill and thickness of the fish.

Steamed Gulf Snapper with Ginger–Green Onion Sauce

SERVES 2 AS A MAIN COURSE

I've seen this aromatic dish many times throughout my life, from celebratory Chinese banquets to the en papillote dishes in the fine dining establishments of my adult life. This version is my absolute favorite, though, with the added depth of sorghum and vinegar rounding out the rich umami presence of the soy sauce. Serve the fish on rimmed plates to contain the sauce and the tableside pour of hot oil; when the oil hits the ginger and green onions, a dramatic sizzle and knockout aroma and flavor is produced. This is best when served with Grilled Okra with Mala Oil (page 26), Fundamental Steamed Rice (page 87), and kimchi. The technique for steaming the fish, a combination of French and Chinese methods, may seem tricky at first, but stick with it, remembering the ultimate goal is to simply seal the fish and aromatics inside a paper pouch.

FOR THE SAUCE:

¼ cup (60 ml) soy sauce

1 tablespoon sorghum syrup

1 clove garlic, minced

2 teaspoons rice vinegar

Ground black pepper

½ teaspoon toasted sesame oil

2 pieces snapper (6 ounces / 170 g each), deboned and skin on (see Note)

Salt and white pepper

2 tablespoons unsalted butter

2 slices lemon

2¼-inch (6 mm) thick slices peeled fresh ginger, plus ½ inch (12 mm) piece peeled fresh ginger, cut into ½ by ¼-inch (12 mm by 6 mm) matchstick strips

¼ cup (25 g) thinly sliced green onions, green and white parts

2 tablespoons canola oil

Preheat oven to 400°F (205°C).

MAKE THE SAUCE: Place the soy sauce, sorghum syrup, garlic, vinegar, ½ teaspoon ground black pepper, and the sesame oil in a small bowl and mix well. Set aside.

Fold an 18 by 13-inch (46 by 33 cm) piece of parchment paper in half to form a crease separating two 9 by 13-inch (23 by 33 cm) areas, then unfold. Season both sides of one piece of fish with salt and white pepper, then place skin side up in the middle of one of the 9 by 13-inch (23 by 33 cm) areas of the unfolded paper that you just created. Place 1 tablespoon butter, 1 lemon slice, and 1 ginger slice on the fish. Fold the other half of the parchment paper over the fish. Starting on one side of the crease, fold about ½ inch (12 mm) of the paper over itself at a rough 45-degree angle to begin sealing the packet. Continue to fold the open edge of the paper in this fashion every 1 inch (2.5 cm) or so until you reach the other open end. Before making the final fold to fully seal the packet, carefully pour about ¼ cup (60 ml) water into the packet, then fold over to make the final seal. Set aside and repeat with another piece of parchment paper and the other piece of fish and place both packets onto a baking sheet. Place in the preheated oven and bake until the parchment is swollen and lightly browned, 8 to 12 minutes.

While the fish is cooking, mix the matchstick strips of ginger and the green onions in a small bowl and set aside.

recipe continues

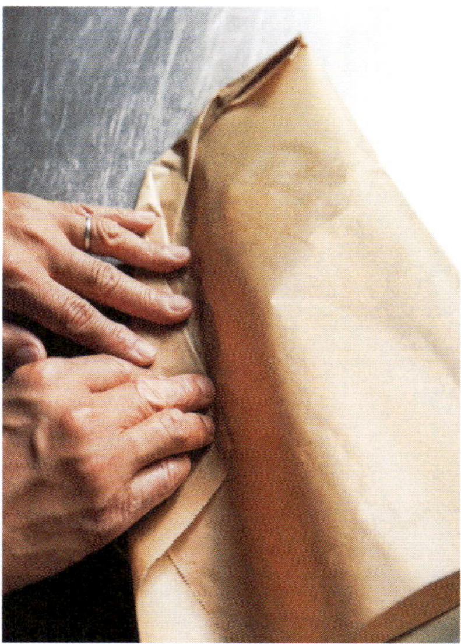

Check if the fish is done by opening one end of its packet and inserting a metal skewer or tip of a paring knife into the middle of the fish for about 5 seconds. Remove and feel the skewer; if it is warm to the touch, the fish is done; if not, reseal the hole and place in the oven for another 1 to 2 minutes.

When the fish is done, remove it from the parchment paper, transfer to two rimmed plates skin side up, and discard the lemon and ginger.

Place the canola oil in a small saucepan over high heat and heat until hot, about 1 minute. Meanwhile, top the fish with the ginger–green onion mixture and spoon 2 to 3 tablespoons of the sauce around the fish. When the oil begins to smoke, use a metal spoon to drizzle half of it over the ginger–green onion mixture of each piece of fish. Serve immediately.

NOTE:

In the South we usually have access to great, fresh Gulf snapper. If you can't find it, any type of red snapper will work, as will black sea bass.

Gulf Shrimp Summer Rolls with Peanut Dipping Sauce

MAKES 4 ROLLS, ENOUGH FOR AN APPETIZER FOR 2

A Vietnamese friend taught me how to make summer rolls while I was a student in Athens, Georgia, but I really started hammering them out during my time as the executive chef of Le Colonial, a Vietnamese restaurant in New York. This recipe is pretty traditional, but what makes it special to me is that the shrimp and peanuts often found in summer rolls have such a strong Southern identity (the Gulf Coast produces delicious shrimp, iconic in dishes like shrimp and grits, while peanuts are one of Georgia's biggest crops, produced so widely that some truffle hunters have found notes of nuttiness in truffles found near peanut trees). I was exposed to these ingredients a lot as a kid, but I didn't fully realize how Georgian these ingredients are until I returned home to Atlanta to open Lazy Betty. If you can source red Gulf shrimp and Georgian peanuts for your kitchen, all the better. It might take a few tries to figure out the rolling technique, but all of your attempts will still taste delicious! Do not skip the peanut dipping sauce—it really adds something extra.

6 cups (1.4 L) ice water, plus 6 cups (1.4 L) cold water

2 tablespoons salt

6 ounces (170 g) medium (36/40) shrimp (about 13 to 15 shrimp), shelled and deveined

8 (9-inch) rice paper wrappers (see Note)

12 large mint leaves

½ cup (45 g) bean sprouts

1 cup (175 g) cooked Vietnamese rice vermicelli

1 large carrot, cut into 2 by ¼-inch (5 cm by 6 mm) matchstick strips (about ½ cup / 60 g)

½ cup (60 g) shredded daikon

1 cup (50 g) shredded romaine lettuce

FOR THE PEANUT DIPPING SAUCE:

1 cup (145 g) roasted, unsalted peanuts

1 tablespoon rice vinegar

⅓ cup (75 ml) hoisin sauce

1 teaspoon minced, peeled fresh ginger

1 teaspoon sriracha sauce (optional)

Fish sauce

Place the ice water in a medium bowl and set aside.

In a 2-quart (2 L) saucepan, combine 6 cups (1.4 L) water and the salt and bring to a boil over high heat. Remove the pan from the heat, add the shrimp, and poach until fully cooked, about 3 minutes. Strain the shrimp and transfer to the ice bath until fully cooled. Remove the shrimp from the ice bath and pat dry with a paper towel. Slice each shrimp in half lengthwise and set aside.

Place the cold water in a bowl. Stack 2 sheets of rice paper wrappers on top of each other (see Note) and submerge them quickly into the cold water (to avoid oversaturating the wrappers, do not let them sit inside the cold water for more than 3 seconds). Place the dipped wrappers on a cutting board and lay 4 pieces of the halved shrimp cut side up on the bottom half of the rice paper. Lay 3 mint leaves across the shrimp, followed by one-quarter of the bean sprouts, vermicelli, carrots, daikon, and lettuce. Fold the sides of the wrapper in toward the fillings, then fold the bottom of the wrapper over the fillings. Continue to roll the wrapper up tightly until a tubular roll is formed and its seal is tight. Repeat until you have formed 4 rolls in total.

recipe continues

MAKE THE PEANUT DIPPING SAUCE: In a blender, combine ½ cup (120 ml) water, the peanuts, vinegar, hoisin sauce, ginger, and sriracha sauce, if using, and blend until smooth. Add fish sauce to taste. Serve the dipping sauce alongside the prepared rolls.

If not being used immediately, the rolls should be stored in an airtight container for up to 3 hours. The sauce can be refrigerated in an airtight container for up to 2 weeks.

NOTE:

A key move here is the double rice paper technique. It makes the rolls far sturdier, allowing for more fillings and a more forgiving rolling process given the delicate, temperamental nature of rice paper. Also, almost any cooked protein would work in place of shrimp (think sliced chicken breast or crispy bacon); just be sure it isn't wet, like pulled pork smothered in sauce. And one more note—from time to time, I also like to hit the peanut sauce with a squirt of sriracha spice, depending on my mood!

Shrimp Toast

SERVES ABOUT 4 AS A SNACK

The promise of delicious shrimp toast at the Oriental Pearl after Chinese lessons on Sundays was more than enough to get me in school on a Sunday as a kid. Along with shu mai, they were my dim sum offering of choice, and though I've done many modern and fancy versions, I always come back to this style. It's a cross between a Japanese sando (with its soft bread generously filled with tasty items) and the traditional Chinese shrimp toast, which is usually open faced and crusted with sesame seeds and deep-fried. Here, we pan-fry the shrimp toast, making it less greasy while keeping all the flavor. If you can find an artisanal loaf of white bread from a local baker, all the better. These toasts are flavorful enough on their own, but you can also dip them in Nuoc Cham (page 248), Red Pepper Marmalade (page 243), or my personal favorite, the sriracha ranch from Crispy Rice Sticks with Sriracha Ranch (page 84).

1 pound (455 g) large (16/20) shrimp (about 16 to 20 shrimp), shelled and deveined, roughly chopped

2 large egg whites

2 teaspoons toasted sesame oil

3 green onions, green and white parts, chopped

1 clove garlic, minced

2 teaspoons minced ginger

Salt and white pepper

8 or 10 slices white bread, crust removed

6 tablespoons (90 ml) canola oil

In a food processor, pulse the shrimp in 3-second spurts until coarsely ground, about 5 pulses.

Add the egg whites, sesame oil, green onions, garlic, and ginger, season with salt and white pepper, and pulse to a chunky paste, roughly another 5 pulses, scraping the side of the bowl down in between pulses.

Divide the paste among 4 or 5 slices of bread and spread it evenly to the edge of each slice. Place another slice of bread on top to make 4 or 5 sandwiches, then slice each sandwich into 4 equal triangles.

In a medium nonstick skillet, heat 2 tablespoons of the canola oil over low heat, then place 4 or 5 of the shrimp toasts in the pan and brown on both sides, flipping frequently, until the shrimp is cooked through, 5 to 7 minutes total (if the shrimp has not cooked through but the bread is getting too dark, you can put the shrimp toast on a baking sheet in a 350°F / 175°C oven for 3 to 4 minutes to cook it through).

Place the cooked toasts on a paper towel–lined plate and repeat until all the toasts are cooked, then serve immediately.

Fish Stew with Black-Eyed Peas, Cumin, and Lemon

SERVES 2 TO 4 AS A MAIN COURSE

Growing up, we celebrated the Western new year with some sparklers and a televised ball drop. The Chinese New Year, on the other hand, was a much more elaborate occasion with lots of extended family. Festivities included red envelopes filled with money for the kids, fireworks, a dragon dance, mahjong, and, of course, an elaborate banquet-style feast, where a whole steamed fish with ginger–green onion soy sauce brought prosperity for the upcoming year. After returning to Atlanta to open Lazy Betty, I discovered the Southern tradition of serving black-eyed peas for luck, and the idea for this lucky new year stew fusing both sides of my roots was born. Serve any time of the year with Lap Cheong Cornbread (page 120) and Grilled Okra with Mala Oil (page 26).

2 tablespoons canola oil

½ cup (60 g) chopped carrots

½ cup (80 g) chopped onion

¼ cup (30 g) chopped celery

4 cloves garlic, thinly sliced

1 large ripe tomato (10 ounces / 280 g), cored and chopped

1 tablespoon ground cumin

1 tablespoon tomato paste

1 cup (240 ml) dry white wine

3 cups (720 ml) Chicken Stock (page 189)

1 cup (200 g) dried black-eyed peas, soaked in cold water overnight, drained

2 sprigs thyme

2 bay leaves

3 ounces (85 g) boneless, skinless catfish fillets, cut into ½-inch (12 mm) cubes

3 ounces (85 g) boneless, skinless snapper fillets, cut into ½-inch (12 mm) cubes

3 ounces (85 g) boneless, skinless sea bass fillets, cut into ½-inch (12 mm) cubes

Zest and juice of 1 lemon (1 tablespoon zest and 3 tablespoons juice)

Salt and black pepper

In a 5-quart (4.7 L) Dutch oven, heat the oil over medium heat. Add the carrots, onion, celery, and garlic and sweat until soft and translucent, 6 to 8 minutes. Add the tomato and cook until it begins to break down, another 1 to 2 minutes. Add the cumin and tomato paste and cook for another 2 minutes, then increase the heat to high and add the white wine. Stir well and reduce the mixture by roughly half, 2 to 4 minutes.

Add the chicken stock, soaked and drained peas, thyme, and bay leaves and bring to a boil, then reduce the heat to maintain a low simmer. Cook, partially covered, for 1 hour, or until the peas are tender, replenishing with water if the liquid reduces excessively.

When the beans are tender, add the fish and lemon zest and simmer for another 2 to 4 minutes, until the fish is just cooked through. Finish the dish with the lemon juice, adjust the seasoning with salt and black pepper, and serve immediately.

Roasted Oysters with Ginger–Green Onion Butter

SERVES 2 TO 4 AS AN APPETIZER

I wasn't a huge fan of oysters for most of my early days, but that changed when I moved back to Atlanta after years away and saw the bounty of beautiful oysters coming from southern waters. With the perspective that only the return home after a long absence can offer, I learned that few things could beat a freshly shucked oyster straight from the ocean, but this recipe offers a different angle, enriching the bivalves with aromatic green onion butter and making them a bit more approachable to those unsure about raw seafood. Source the freshest oysters you can, from local waters if possible, and serve them with a warm, fresh baguette on the side to sop up all that good, briny butter left pooled in the shells.

1½ teaspoons minced garlic

1½ teaspoons minced, peeled fresh ginger

2 green onions, light green to green parts only, minced

4 ounces (115 g) unsalted butter, softened

1 cup (10 ounces / 280 g) sea salt

6 oysters, scrubbed and shucked

Preheat the oven's broiler to high.

In a bowl, mix the garlic, ginger, green onions, and butter until thoroughly combined and set aside.

In another bowl, mix the salt with 2 tablespoons water. Divide the mixture into 6 mounds on a baking sheet and top each mound with a freshly shucked oyster.

Top each oyster with roughly 1 teaspoon of the butter mixture (refrigerate excess butter for up to 1 month for another use, such as finishing a fried rice dish or stir-fried noodles). Place under the preheated broiler and cook until the butter is melted and bubbling and the oysters are warmed through, 2 to 3 minutes. Serve immediately.

Fresh Shucked Oysters with Ponzu and Wasabi

SERVES 2 AS AN APPETIZER

In this recipe, you get to enjoy the freshness of a raw oyster with a sneaky taste of a Southern grill via the sorghum syrup and liquid smoke in my take on the traditional Japanese sauce known as *ponzu*. The flavors meld and develop complexity with a long rest time of one week, but you can use the sauce immediately if you are in a pinch. Also note that this batch will leave plenty of ponzu available for other recipes, so use it as a finished sauce as described here, or as a marinade for grilled or roasted fish and meats.

FOR THE PONZU:

½ cup (120 ml) soy sauce

½ cup (120 ml) lemon juice (about 4 large lemons)

¼ cup (60 ml) lime juice (about 2 limes)

¼ cup (60 ml) yuzu juice (if not available, substitute with additional lime juice)

2 tablespoons mirin

½ cup (¼ ounce / 7 g) katsuobushi (bonito flakes)

1 piece kombu

1 tablespoon sorghum syrup

½ teaspoon liquid smoke (see Notes)

6 oysters, scrubbed

Wasabi paste

MAKE THE PONZU: In a pint-size (480 ml) mason jar (or other container with a tight-fitting lid), combine the soy sauce, lemon juice, lime juice, yuzu juice, mirin, katsuobushi, kombu, sorghum syrup, and liquid smoke and shake well. Refrigerate the sauce in the sealed jar for at least 1 week to let the flavors develop.

When ready to serve, shuck the oysters, top with a small dab of wasabi paste, and drizzle 5 to 6 drops of the ponzu sauce on top. Serve immediately. Leftover sauce can be refrigerated for up to 2 months.

NOTES:

This recipe contains some unique ingredients that can be found in Asian markets. Yuzu is a citrus fruit that tastes like a lemon with a touch of orange, and mirin is a sweet, low alcohol wine used widely in Japanese cooking. Katsuobushi and kombu are products of the sea: The former consists of thin shavings of dried, smoked bonito tuna, while the latter is a thick kelp, both of which bring a deep umami quality to dishes.

Liquid smoke, on the other hand, offers an easy way to bring a highly concentrated smoke flavor when you're short on time, don't want to build a fire, or don't want ingredients to be exposed to heat.

Fried Catfish with Sauce Chirizu

SERVES 2 AS A MAIN COURSE

Ironically, this dish wasn't inspired by the cornmeal-fried catfish frequently encountered in the South. In fact, this tempura-battered fish fry was taught to me by my Japanese friend Chef Shin Takagi when I staged in his restaurant Zeniya in Kanazawa, Japan, and while we were paired up on *The Final Table* on Netflix. My version is slightly different in that I include wasabi in the sauce to add a dynamic, peppery spice. All you really need for the tempura batter is flour and water to make an ethereal, delicate coating, something I learned while working in Japan through my late twenties. Keep the batter cold to allow a bit more frying time before it turns golden brown, letting the fish cook through, and to keep that coating light, avoid overmixing it, something made simpler by using chopsticks to stir the water and low-gluten cake flour. As for the citrusy, spicy chirizu, it's my take on a traditional Japanese dipping sauce that I think is good on everything. The grated daikon makes it even more special, giving the sauce body to latch on to whatever is being dipped in it. The final result resembles fish sticks, and is a dish my young daughter loves eating, always asking for more.

FOR THE SAUCE:

⅓ cup (75 g) finely grated daikon

1 teaspoon togarashi (see Note)

2 green onions, green and white parts, minced

1 teaspoon wasabi

¼ cup (60 ml) soy sauce

1 tablespoon lemon juice

FOR THE TEMPURA BATTER:

1 cup (130 g) cake flour or all-purpose flour

2 cups (480 ml) ice water

½ cup (70 g) ice cubes

Canola oil, for deep-frying

1 cup (130 g) cake flour

1 pound (455 g) catfish fillets, cut into 3 by 1-inch (7.5 by 2.5 cm) strips

Salt

MAKE THE SAUCE: Combine the daikon, togarashi, green onions, wasabi, soy sauce, and lemon juice in a medium bowl. Mix well and set aside.

MAKE THE TEMPURA BATTER: Place 1 cup (130 g) cake flour in a large bowl and slowly pour in the ice water while stirring with a pair of chopsticks (place a damp towel under the bowl to prevent it from moving). Once fully incorporated, stop mixing (overmixing will develop the flour's gluten and make the coating less airy and crisp when cooked). Refrigerate the batter, uncovered, until ready to proceed.

Set up a frying station. In a large, heavy pot set up with an oil thermometer, heat 2 inches (5 cm) canola oil over high heat until it reaches 350°F (175°C). Have a spider and paper towel–lined plate ready.

Place 1 cup (130 g) cake flour on a baking sheet. Dredge each piece of catfish in the flour, shaking off any excess, then set on a plate. Once all of the fish is dredged, add the ice to the batter.

Working in batches as necessary to avoid overcrowding the oil and dropping the oil temperature, dip a piece of fish into the batter to fully coat it, then gently lay it into the oil. Fry until golden brown, about 3 minutes, then use a spider to remove the fish from the oil, shaking off excess oil, and set on the paper towel–lined plate.

Season with salt and serve immediately with the sauce chirizu on the side for dipping.

NOTE:

Togarashi is a Japanese spice mix usually consisting of chili, orange zest, seaweed, and sesame seeds, easily found in Asian markets or online.

Pickled Gulf Shrimp with Coconut Milk

SERVES 2 AS AN APPETIZER

A light, aromatic shrimp ceviche is the perfect summer snack. It wasn't until I returned to the South that I fully realized the similarities between the ceviche we made at Le Bernardin in New York and the pickled shrimp I knew in Georgia. Both use acid to "cook" the shrimp or fish, preserving it and making it safe to eat without applying heat. Here, I utilize the Southeast Asian flavors of ginger, chile, and coconut milk with sweet Gulf shrimp, best served cold as an appetizer alongside good, crusty bread.

8 ounces (225 g) medium (36/40) shrimp (about 18 to 20 shrimp), shelled and deveined

¾ cup (180 ml) rice vinegar

¼ cup (30 g) thinly sliced red onion

1 lime, sliced into thin rounds

¼ cup (60 ml) canola oil

3 sprigs cilantro

2 sprigs Thai basil

1-inch (2.5 cm) piece fresh ginger, peeled and crushed with the side of a chef's knife

1 red Fresno chile (optional)

½ teaspoon sugar

½ teaspoon salt

⅓ cup (75 ml) unsweetened coconut milk

In a quart-size (960 ml) mason jar (or other container with a tight-fitting lid), combine the shrimp and vinegar and shake well. Refrigerate for 20 minutes, then add the onion, lime, oil, cilantro, basil, ginger, chile (if using), sugar, and salt, shake well, and refrigerate in the sealed jar overnight.

The next day, add the coconut milk, shake well, and let the flavors marry for about 30 minutes or up to 1 week before serving.

Seared Scallops with Jasmine-Buttermilk Risotto

SERVES 2 AS A MAIN COURSE

I love simple steamed rice, but creamy, al dente risotto is another favorite. This recipe uses the traditional technique of gradually adding hot stock to rice while constantly stirring to allow the starches to create a creamy texture, but I've switched to a fragrant, long-grain jasmine rice, and upped the flavors with assertive ingredients like buttermilk, lime, and ginger. Preserve the starch by not washing the rice beforehand, and let it absorb the stock slowly—it will ask for more liquid when a wooden spoon dragged across the bottom of the pan leaves a dry streak. Aim for al dente—not grainy—rice, and don't dump too much stock in at the end lest you overcook it. The scallops are a quick way to elevate the dish to an elegant dinner for two. Look for big, juicy sea scallops rather than tiny bay scallops.

FOR THE RICE:

1 quart (960 ml) Chicken Stock (page 189)

1 tablespoon unsalted butter

1 tablespoon finely chopped shallots

1 teaspoon minced, peeled fresh ginger

1 cup (185 g) jasmine rice or other long-grain rice

¼ cup (60 ml) buttermilk

Juice of ½ lime (1 tablespoon)

1 tablespoon finely chopped cilantro

Salt and white pepper

FOR THE SCALLOPS:

2 tablespoons canola oil

6 U/10 sea scallops (10 to 12 ounces / 280 to 340 g)

Salt and white pepper

Lime wedges

MAKE THE RICE: In a small saucepan, bring the stock to a boil over high heat, then reduce the heat to low to keep it warm.

Meanwhile, melt the butter in a skillet over low heat, then add the shallots and ginger and cook, stirring occasionally with a wooden spoon, until translucent, 1 to 2 minutes. Add the rice to the skillet and stir to coat it with the butter for 2 minutes. Add ½ cup (120 ml) of the hot stock to the skillet and stir constantly until most of the liquid has been absorbed, about 2 minutes, then add another ½ cup (120 ml) of the stock and repeat this process until the rice is creamy and al dente. This process should take about 12 to 14 minutes; heat more stock if needed.

Remove the skillet from the heat and stir in the buttermilk, lime juice, and cilantro and season with salt and white pepper. Cover the skillet to keep the rice warm and set aside.

MAKE THE SCALLOPS: Remove the tough crescent-shaped "foot" from the side of each scallop and discard. Pat the scallops dry with a paper towel and season with salt and white pepper. In a skillet, heat the canola oil over medium-high heat until thin wisps of smoke form, then place the scallops into the pan evenly, gently pressing them into the pan to ensure full contact between the scallop and the pan. Let cook without moving until deeply golden brown, 2 to 3 minutes, then reduce the heat to low and flip each scallop to kiss the other side with heat for about 30 seconds, and then remove the skillet from the heat.

Divide the rice between 2 plates, then top each plate with 3 scallops and 1 lime wedge and serve immediately.

Sorghum and Soy Marinated Black Cod

SERVES 2 AS A MAIN COURSE

I first had Nobu's famous version of this dish while I lived in New York, and since have riffed on it in many different ways, but never has it been better than when I was able to use black cod freshly caught by the fishermen near Pillar Point Harbor while driving with my in-laws from San Francisco to Pescadero. I had recent experiments with Chinese-style tea-smoked dishes on my mind, and, recalling that Chick-fil-A brines their chicken in pickle juice, I thought I'd try another nontraditional marinade. So, during that California visit, tasked with cooking fresh fish for the family, I included Southern black tea, which not only gives the dish a complementary depth of flavor, but also gives the fish a nice amber color. This is a versatile dish, just as delicious fresh from the broiler over steamed rice with Stir-Fried Watercress (page 56) as it is served cold as part of a bento-style lunch box. Or make it into wraps with lettuce leaves, steamed sushi rice, and various pickled vegetables, as my daughter loves.

2 pieces black cod (sablefish) fillets (6 ounces / 170 g each), cleaned, skinned, and deboned (see Note)

FOR THE MARINADE:

1 clove garlic, minced

½ teaspoon minced, peeled fresh ginger

1 tablespoon sorghum syrup

2 tablespoons light soy sauce

1 tablespoon dark soy sauce

¼ teaspoon white pepper

¼ cup (60 ml) cold, unsweetened black tea

1 tablespoon white miso

½ teaspoon toasted sesame oil

1 tablespoon canola oil

Place the fish in a zip-top plastic bag and set aside.

MAKE THE MARINADE: In a medium bowl, combine all the ingredients and whisk until fully incorporated. Pour into the zip-top bag, then seal the bag, pressing out as much air as possible and making sure the fish is submerged in the marinade. Marinate for at least 30 minutes or up to 4 hours, flipping the bag halfway through the marinating time to ensure even coverage (refrigerate if marinating longer than 30 minutes, and remove the fish from the refrigerator roughly 30 minutes before you are ready to proceed).

When ready to proceed, preheat the broiler and line a baking sheet with aluminum foil. Rub the foil with the canola oil, focusing on where you will place the fish. Remove the fish from the marinade and pat with a paper towel to remove excess marinade, then put on the prepared pan, making sure the fillets do not touch each other.

Place the fish in the oven and broil for 6 to 9 minutes, taking care not to burn the fish, until a metal skewer inserted in the middle of the fish for 5 seconds is warm to the touch. Serve immediately.

NOTE:

Black cod, also known as *sablefish*, is an entirely different species than cod, which will not provide the fatty richness of sablefish and should not be used as a substitute in this recipe. If sablefish isn't available, Chilean sea bass works well; use salmon if a white-fleshed fish isn't available.

CHAPTER 5

Beef

Le Bernardin

ABOVE: Ron with Eric Ripert on his last day at Le Bernadin.

I spent nearly a decade at New York City's Le Bernardin working my way up from a cook to the creative director, and aside from my mother, nothing has had a larger impact on me professionally. I met people from places of the world I didn't experience back in the kitchens of Hunan Village: new friends from France, India, Norway, Portugal, and South Africa; people who lived in fancy apartments spanning entire floors of doorman buildings in Manhattan; people who lived six people to a tiny two-bedroom apartment.

Diversity didn't stop with the staff. The restaurant itself was French, but we always had such a worldly, modern menu, which brought me some challenges during my time at Le Bernardin. Internally, I felt conflicted. Here we were, in this incredibly diverse city, with a menu nodding to all corners of the world, but so many of the dishes I was developing leaned Asian, and more specifically, Chinese. I went to Chef Eric Ripert, one of the world's best, and his advice? *Don't worry about it.* He taught me to listen to my inner chef and let the menu fall into place, and that if I resisted what I was naturally gravitating to too much, I'd risk constricting my full creativity. Here I was, a twenty-eight-year-old chef at one of the most prestigious restaurants in the world, being told by the chef that my style of food *was* good enough and *was* wanted. After growing up being laughed at and mocked for being Chinese, it was here, on the grandest stage, that I finally felt valued and praised.

Plus, it was at Le Bernardin that I truly learned how to carry myself as a real professional. Chef Ripert never gave me any direct one-on-one lessons on this; it just sort of soaked in as I watched him interact with everyone on staff. He treated first days stages the same way he treated twenty-year veterans of the restaurant: kindly and fairly. And it didn't stop with the staff; guests got the family treatment, as did the myriad film and media producers, photographers, and other industry-adjacent professionals that came through. Ever see him on camera? He's *exactly* the same in person. Kind, humble, generous. And he's a champion of abolishing the old school, cut-throat ways of running a kitchen. Here's a guy who, from his perch atop the restaurant world, could dunk on anyone he wanted to, but he never did, relating to people up and down the food chain, and despite all the amazing culinary lessons he taught me, it is these lessons in kindness that have gotten me furthest in life.

ABOVE: Dishes Ron helped develop at Le Bernadin: beef tartare with caviar and dashi gelée (top left), pan-roasted monkfish and sauce romesco (top right), grilled escolar and Wagyu with stuffed endive (bottom left), and crab choux farcis with chili crab broth (bottom right).

Grilled Mandarin Beef Ribs

SERVES 2 AS A MAIN COURSE

When my brother got married a few years ago, my father prepared his version of these ribs for over sixty people, including our Chinese-Malaysian aunts and uncles, Southern family and friends, even my sister-in-law's family from Sweden. Everyone loved it! We always called this style of beef rib "Mandarin" at my mom's restaurant Hunan Village when I was a kid, but they are actually quite similar to the Korean barbecued short ribs known as *kalbi*, something I realized eating late night drunk food in New York's Koreatown after a killer night of service at Le Bernardin. Drunk or not, this dish is easy to love, especially when eaten with a bowl of Fundamental Steamed Rice (page 87) and Crushed Garlic and Cucumber Salad (page 39).

FOR THE MARINADE:

2 cups (480 ml) light soy sauce

1½ cups (360 ml) sorghum syrup

2 tablespoons sesame seeds

½ teaspoon ground white pepper

1 bunch green onions, green and white parts thinly sliced

1 tablespoon toasted sesame oil

2-inch (5 cm) piece fresh ginger, cut crosswise into ¼-inch (6 mm) slices and crushed with the side of a chef's knife

3 cloves garlic, crushed with the side of a chef's knife

1 pound (455 g) beef short ribs, cross cut on the bones, meat pounded ¼-inch (6 mm) thin (see Notes)

MAKE THE MARINADE: In a large bowl, thoroughly combine all of the marinade ingredients and ½ cup (120 ml) water. Place the ribs in a zip-top plastic bag and add enough marinade to coat them (excess marinade can be frozen for later use). Seal the bag, pressing out as much air as possible and making sure the beef is submerged in the marinade. Marinate for at least 1 hour or up to 6 hours, flipping the bag halfway through the marinating time to ensure even coverage (refrigerate if marinating longer than 1 hour, and remove the beef from the refrigerator roughly 1 hour before you are ready to proceed).

Preheat your clean and seasoned grill over high heat (see Notes).

Remove the beef from the marinade, gently shaking the ribs to remove excess marinade. Place the beef on the hot grill and cook for 2 minutes per side, turning once dark grill marks appear, for medium-rare or until desired doneness. Serve immediately.

NOTES:

Beef ribs of this style are also known as *flanken style* or sometimes *Korean style*. In appearance, they almost look like a big fat piece of bacon with three small pieces of bone. Look for ribs with good marbling and no oxidization—the meat should be deeply red. When pounding the ribs, be gentle so as not to tear the meat.

Seasoning your grill simply means to get it ready for cooking. Heat it to the desired cooking temperature, then use a strong wire brush to remove any sediment remaining from previous uses. Lightly soak a paper towel or wadded-up newspaper with canola oil and use tongs to rub the oil all over the grill grates to give it a clean, slick surface for cooking.

Mandarin Beef and Papaya Salad with Roasted Peanuts

SERVES 2 AS A MAIN COURSE

Morning Glory, a restaurant in Hoi An, Vietnam, has my favorite version of this salad, but their method is quite elaborate and uses ingredients like banana blossoms, dehydrated shrimp, and local herbs that can be challenging to find stateside. I've simplified things without cutting back on flavor, using easier to find ingredients, including the peaches my home state is known for instead of mangos. While Morning Glory makes their own fried shallots and garlic, you can just pick some up in an Asian market or online and use the extra anywhere you want a crunchy, salty bit of allium flavor. For the beef, I like to use the Grilled Mandarin Beef Ribs (page 159), which makes the dish heartier and adds a smoky flavor that really elevates the salad. You could also swap the ribs out for the Lemongrass Pork Chops (page 104) or Pickled Gulf Shrimp with Coconut Milk (page 149), if that tickles your fancy!

2 cups (300 g) sliced green papaya, peeled, seeded, and cut into thin strips roughiy 1 inch (2.5 cm) long by ¼ inch (6 mm) wide

Salt

8 ounces (225 g) Grilled Mandarin Beef Ribs (page 159)

1 peach, cut into thin strips roughly 1 inch (2.5 cm) long by ¼ inch (6 mm) wide

1 small carrot, peeled and cut into thin strips roughly 1 inch (2.5 cm) long by ¼ inch (6 mm) wide

¼ medium red onion, cut into thin strips roughly 1 inch (2.5 cm) long by ¼ inch (6 mm) wide

½ medium Granny Smith apple, cut into thin strips roughly 1 inch (2.5 cm) long by ¼ inch (6 mm) wide

¼ cup (25 g) bean sprouts

¼ cup (4 g) cilantro leaves

¼ cup (4 g) Thai basil leaves

¼ cup (4 g) mint leaves

¼ cup (60 ml) Nuoc Cham (page 248)

¼ lemongrass stalk, top half and outer leaves removed, finely minced (1 tablespoon)

1 teaspoon minced fresh ginger

White pepper

2 tablespoons fried shallots, homemade or store-bought (see Note on page 217)

2 tablespoons fried garlic, homemade or store-bought (see Note on page 217)

1 tablespoon roasted peanuts

In a medium bowl, toss the papaya with a pinch of salt, then set aside.

Remove the cooked beef from its bones and cut into thin slices, then set aside.

Place the salted green papaya, peach, carrot, red onion, apple, bean sprouts, cilantro, Thai basil, and mint in a large bowl.

In a small bowl, stir the nuoc cham, lemongrass, and ginger together, then pour over the vegetables. Season with salt and white pepper and gently toss.

Divide the salad between two bowls, then divide the reserved beef between the two bowls. Top with the fried shallots, fried garlic, and peanuts and serve immediately.

Hot Garlic

Stir-Fried Beef with Fermented Black Beans and Collard Greens

SERVES 4 AS A MAIN COURSE

I learned the difference between velveting and simple frying from an old school chef who worked for me in New York, someone I actually called "big brother" in Chinese as a term of endearment and respect. After cooking meat in the deep fryer, he pulled a beautifully caramelized, completely changed product from the oil. It didn't look like a typical piece of deep-fried meat, like a chicken wing or Southern-style buttermilk fried chicken—it had become quite tender and had a velvet-like coating that soaked up sauce. Turns out the meat had been more than merely deep-fried. It had been velveted before frying, one technique before another, and it was a step that made the whole thing better as the meat became absorbent and tender, ready to receive the sauce he then finished it in.

Think of velveting as marination *plus*. It's a crucial step in Chinese cooking wherein an ingredient, usually a protein, is manipulated before stir-frying. The key components of velveting include adding flavor like soy sauce and spices, a starch such as cornstarch (to form a velvet-like coating on the protein to which sauce can easily adhere), and a tenderizer like baking soda, used only if needed on a tough cut of meat. We use the velveting technique in this recipe, as well as on Lemongrass Pork Chops (page 104) and Salt and Pepper Chicken-Fried Steak (page 175).

Velveting is key in this easy, high-payoff one-pan dish. It marinates and tenderizes the beef and creates that outer coating allowing it to absorb the sauce as it is stir-fried with the deeply flavorful umami bombs known as *fermented black beans* (see Pantry, page 17) and hearty collard greens. This dish needs no accompaniment other than a bowl of Fundamental Steamed Rice (page 87), and maybe a dollop of your favorite chili crunch.

FOR THE MARINADE:

1 teaspoon black pepper

1 teaspoon ground cumin

½ teaspoon sugar

½ teaspoon salt

1 tablespoon cornstarch

½ teaspoon baking soda

1 teaspoon canola oil

1 teaspoon soy sauce

8 ounces (225 g) flank steak, cut into 1 by ¼-inch (2.5 cm by 6 mm) slices

FOR THE SAUCE:

3 tablespoons (45 ml) Chicken Stock (page 189)

½ teaspoon cornstarch

1 teaspoon rice vinegar

1 teaspoon toasted sesame oil

1 tablespoon oyster sauce

1 tablespoon soy sauce

2 teaspoons sugar

1 tablespoon Shaoxing cooking wine

2 tablespoons canola oil, plus more as needed

3 cloves garlic, minced

1 tablespoon minced, peeled fresh ginger

1 tablespoon fermented black beans, rinsed under warm water for 10 seconds

½ cup (60 g) sliced red onion

8 ounces (225 g) collard greens, cleaned and chopped into 1-inch (2.5 cm) pieces (2 cups loosely packed)

Salt and black pepper

recipe continues

MARINATE THE BEEF: Place the black pepper, cumin, sugar, salt, cornstarch, baking soda, canola oil, and soy sauce in a large bowl and mix well. Add the flank steak, mix well, and let the steak marinate and velvet for at least 10 minutes or up to 4 hours, refrigerating if marinating over 1 hour.

MAKE THE SAUCE: Combine the stock, cornstarch, rice vinegar, sesame oil, oyster sauce, soy sauce, sugar, and Shaoxing cooking wine in a small bowl and mix well. Set aside.

In a large skillet or wok over medium-high heat, heat the 2 tablespoons canola oil until it begins to smoke. Add the beef to the pan and cook, stirring frequently (stir-frying), until seared and dark brown, 1 to 2 minutes, then remove the beef from the pan.

Remove excess oil from the pan (keeping about 1 tablespoon of fat in the pan, replenishing if need be) and return the pan to medium-high heat. When the pan is smoking again, add the garlic and ginger and stir constantly to infuse them into the oil until they are lightly browned, about 10 seconds, taking care not to burn them. Add the fermented black beans to the pan and stir-fry for about another 5 seconds, until aromatic. Add the onions and cook for another 30 seconds, or until beginning to char, then return the beef to the pan and cook for another 45 seconds while stirring frequently.

Stir the sauce mixture well, then add it and the collard greens to the pan and bring the sauce up to a simmer and thicken, 30 to 60 seconds. Stir well and remove the pan from the heat. Taste and adjust the seasoning with salt and black pepper and serve immediately.

Pho Broth with Beef Bones

SERVES 2 AS A MAIN COURSE

Although I was raised in a Chinese kitchen, had lots of Southern cooking influence since my early days, and have experienced so much French cuisine in school and professionally, Vietnamese food has been very near and dear to me from the get-go. A favorite of mine is pho, the cleansing, restorative Vietnamese noodle soup made with a broth loaded with aromatic spices and rich beef bones and oxtails. The evolution of my pho recipe started during my time as executive chef at Le Colonial in New York City, but some of my favorite pho memories are from when I was a kid. After my Chinese classes as a kid, a big bowl of steaming pho was the go-to meal at the now closed Pho 22, down the street from the school in "Asian Square," a strip mall just off the international food strip known as Buford Highway in Atlanta (see page 124). I'd sit down to the steamy bowl and pile bean sprouts and fragrant Thai basil on top of the noodles swimming in the broth before slurping it all up. I enjoy all kinds of noodles for this dish, from simple macaroni to alkaline ramen noodles, but ultimately, traditional Vietnamese rice noodles will always be my favorite—look for a package of fresh rice pho noodles, as they'll make the prep much easier and faster since you won't have to rehydrate them. This recipe gives you a strong broth base on which to build your bowl, and I suggest adding the toppings a young Ron Hsu enjoyed way back when, included here, but it's really up to you. Sometimes I add pulled pork, smoked chicken, or even smoked brisket from a local barbecue joint for a fun play on the brisket commonly found in traditional bowls of pho.

recipe continues

- 3 pounds (1.4 kg) beef bones (see Notes)
- 8 ounces (225 g) oxtails
- Two 3-inch (7.5 cm) cinnamon sticks
- 1 teaspoon whole white peppercorns
- 1 teaspoon whole Szechuan peppercorns
- 1 tablespoon whole black cardamom pods
- 3 star anise pods
- 1 yellow onion, halved
- 3 cloves garlic, crushed with side of a cleaver
- Two 2-inch (5 cm) pieces fresh ginger, crushed with the side of a cleaver
- 2 stalks lemongrass, crushed with the side of a cleaver
- 2 green onions, white parts left whole and green parts thinly sliced on the bias and reserved for garnish
- 5 cilantro stems
- ⅓ cup (75 ml) fish sauce, more or less if desired
- 1 tablespoon rock sugar, more or less if desired
- Salt and white pepper
- Cooked noodles, bean sprouts, Thai basil, cilantro, sliced chiles, lime wedges, sriracha, hoisin sauce, for serving

In a large, lidded stockpot, combine the bones and oxtails with 2 gallons (7.5 L) water and bring to a boil over high heat. When a boil is reached, remove the pot from the heat, then strain and discard the liquid (see Notes). Replace with another 2 gallons (7.5 L) water and place over high heat.

Meanwhile, in a skillet, toast the cinnamon sticks, white peppercorns, Szechuan peppercorns, cardamom pods, and star anise over medium-low heat until quite fragrant, 2 to 3 minutes, then add the spices to the stockpot.

Wipe any residue from the skillet with a paper towel, then heat the skillet over high heat until hot and starting to smoke, 2 to 3 minutes. Place the onion halves in the pan, cut side down (without oil), and leave until dark brown, 4 to 5 minutes.

Transfer the onions to the stockpot and add the garlic, ginger, lemongrass, green onion whites, and cilantro stems. When the liquid comes to a boil, note the level of liquid in the pot and reduce the heat to maintain a low simmer. Partially cover the pot with its lid (about 30 percent) and cook for 8 hours or up to overnight, replenishing the water to maintain its original level as needed.

Strain the broth through a sieve and discard the solids. Stir in the fish sauce and rock sugar and season with salt and white pepper. Taste, and adjust the seasoning as desired. Serve the hot broth in large bowls with cooked noodles, bean sprouts, the reserved green onion greens, Thai basil, cilantro, sliced chiles, lime wedges, sriracha, and hoisin sauce.

Any leftover broth may be frozen for up to 3 months.

NOTES:

Blanching the bones and discarding the first batch of liquid is a way to remove any impurities in the bones, "cleaning" them for the second boil during which all their flavor will be extracted. Look for a variety of beef bones, including knuckles and marrow bones that have been split and cut into smaller pieces for maximum extraction of their richness and flavor.

If you're really ambitious, you can save the bones after draining the pho broth and use them to make a remouillage, a less flavorful but still-better-than-water stock. The word itself means "rewetting" in French and is a testament to the squeezing water from a stone spirit of the process: Place the bones back in a stockpot with some aromatics like chopped onions, carrots, celery, and a few bay leaves, cover with water, and simmer again for a few hours. Strain out the solids and there you have it: a remouillage that can be used pretty much anywhere stock is called for, and even in place of water when making a stock for an extra boost of flavor.

Kare Kare Oxtail Stew

SERVES 4 AS A MAIN COURSE

This classic Filipino stew is one of my favorites. Enriched with peanut butter and traditionally made with oxtails, it also works well with pork shoulder or even chicken thighs in a pinch. Any peanut butter will work—but all the better if you can find one from my home state of Georgia. Serve this stew with Garlic Fried Rice with Chicken Fat (page 74) or stone-ground grits.

2 tablespoons annatto seeds (see Note)

1½ pounds (680 g) oxtails

1 tablespoon canola oil

1-inch (2.5 cm) piece fresh ginger, peeled and thinly sliced

5 cloves garlic, thinly sliced

3 shallots, peeled and thinly sliced

1 teaspoon coarsely ground black pepper

1 quart (960 ml) Chicken Stock (page 189)

3 tablespoons fish sauce

1 cup (260 g) smooth peanut butter

4½ teaspoons cornstarch

6 pieces okra, sliced into ¼-inch (6 mm) pieces

8 ounces (225 g) turnip or collard greens, cleaned and chopped (2 cups loosely packed)

In a small saucepan, combine the annatto seeds with 1 cup (240 ml) water and bring to a boil. Immediately remove the pan from the heat and set aside to allow the annatto to infuse into the water for 10 minutes, then strain and set the liquid aside, discarding the seeds.

Meanwhile, in a large saucepan, cover the oxtails with cold water and bring to a boil over high heat. Once a boil is reached, strain and discard the liquid (for more on this blanching process, see Note, page 167). Rinse the pot and set the oxtail aside.

Place the saucepan over medium heat and add the oil. When oil is hot and begins to shimmer, add the ginger, garlic, and shallots and cook, stirring occasionally, until translucent, 4 to 6 minutes. Add the black pepper, stir, and cook for 30 seconds, then add the stock, fish sauce, and reserved oxtail to the pot. Bring to a simmer, then reduce the heat to maintain a simmer and cook, loosely covered, for 1½ hours, replenishing the liquid with water to maintain the original level as needed.

Add about half of the annatto liquid to get a nice amber color (use more or less as desired), refrigerating any remaining annatto liquid indefinitely for another use, and stir in the peanut butter until incorporated. In a small bowl, whisk the cornstarch with 2 tablespoons water, then stir the stew to get the liquid moving, add the cornstarch slurry, and continue stirring until completely incorporated. Stir in the okra and greens, bring the stew back to a simmer for 3 to 4 minutes until the okra is slightly tender and the greens wilted, and serve immediately. Leftovers are fantastic—store them tightly sealed and refrigerated for up to 1 week, or frozen for up to 2 months.

NOTE:

Annatto, commonly found in cheeses, as it is used to color them yellow or orange, and in Mexican achiote paste, is used here sheerly to impart a deep amber color to the stew.

Meatloaf with Shiitake Mushrooms

SERVES 4 AS A MAIN COURSE

One of my mom's go-to dishes for me, her young, budding chef, was Salisbury steak, and this meatloaf, rich with the deep, earthy flavor of shiitake mushrooms. It was an easy way to sneak vegetables into my meals. I use the same trick with my daughter, serving it atop mashed potatoes or steamed white rice; don't forget to serve ketchup on the side, if desired!

2 tablespoons canola oil

2 cups (170 g) finely chopped shiitake mushrooms (stems removed)

½ cup (80 g) finely chopped onion

½ cup (65 g) finely chopped carrots

4 cloves garlic, minced

½ cup (40 g) panko

½ cup (120 ml) whole milk

2 pounds (910 g) ground beef

2 eggs, beaten

1 teaspoon salt

1 teaspoon ground black pepper

1 teaspoon Worcestershire sauce

FOR THE GLAZE:

½ cup (120 g) ketchup

1 tablespoon soy sauce

In a skillet, heat the oil over low heat. Add the mushrooms, onions, carrots, and garlic and cook until soft but not browned, 5 to 7 minutes. Remove from the heat and allow to cool for about 10 minutes.

Meanwhile, in a small bowl, combine the panko and milk and set aside to allow the panko to fully absorb the milk while the vegetables finish cooling.

Line a baking sheet with aluminum foil and preheat the oven to 350°F (175°C).

In a large bowl, mix the ground beef, eggs, salt, black pepper, Worcestershire sauce, soaked panko, and cooled vegetables with your hands until fully incorporated. On the foil-lined baking sheet, form the meatloaf mixture into an 8 by 4-inch (20 by 10 cm) loaf, then bake the meatloaf until a meat thermometer inserted in the center of the loaf reaches 150°F (65°C), 35 to 40 minutes.

MEANWHILE, MAKE THE GLAZE: In a small bowl, mix the ketchup and soy sauce. When the meatloaf reaches 150°F (65°C), remove it from the oven and adjust the oven control to broil. Spread half of the glaze over the meatloaf, then return the loaf to the oven and broil until the glaze is bubbling and lacquered, 3 to 4 minutes.

Remove the loaf from the broiler and let it rest for 10 minutes, then slice and serve immediately with the remaining glaze alongside. Refrigerate leftover meatloaf, uncut, for up to 3 days.

Barbecue Brisket and Rice Cake Stir-Fry

SERVES 1 TO 2 AS A MAIN COURSE

Growing up, my second favorite beef dish at Hunan Village (after the Grilled Mandarin Beef Ribs, page 159) was beef and broccoli, and that's still a dish I order when getting neighborhood Chinese food. This dish has roots in that nostalgic love, using tender smoked brisket instead of velveted beef (see page 163) for a quick, tasty alternative due to its similar texture and smoky flavor. Thin Broccolini brings a sleeker crunch to the dish than the usual large broccoli florets, and Chinese rice cakes, also known as *nian gao*, carry the flavor of the sauce and add a delightful chew (you can also use Korean tteok, most well-known as a component of the dish tteokbokki). You can easily multiply this recipe to make more as desired. Just remember to avoid overcrowding your pan, cooking in batches as needed to ensure the vegetables and sauce cook quickly. This will keep your vegetables from getting too soft.

Getting wok hei on this stir-fry by using a real-deal wok (see Note) really complements the smokiness of the barbecue, but if your home kitchen isn't equipped with one, we've included instructions for using a skillet. Enjoy this dish on its own, with a side of Fundamental Steamed Rice (page 87), over grits, or with a hunk of Lap Cheong Cornbread (page 120).

FOR THE SAUCE:

1 tablespoon Shaoxing cooking wine

½ teaspoon coarsely ground black pepper

1 tablespoon oyster sauce

½ cup (120 ml) Chicken Stock (page 189)

1 teaspoon cornstarch

1 teaspoon toasted sesame oil

1 teaspoon soy sauce

Salt

2 tablespoons canola oil

1½ teaspoons minced garlic

1½ teaspoons minced, peeled fresh ginger

½ medium red onion, cut into 1-inch (2.5 cm) semicircles

1 bunch Broccolini (about 8 ounces / 225 g), cut into 1-inch (2.5 cm) pieces and large florets split in half

1 cup (100 g) rice cakes

8 ounces (225 g) smoked brisket from your local barbecue spot, sliced ¼ inch (6 mm) thick

MAKE THE SAUCE: In a small bowl, stir the Shaoxing cooking wine, black pepper, oyster sauce, chicken stock, cornstarch, sesame oil, soy sauce, and salt to taste until combined and set aside.

In a large wok or skillet, heat the canola oil over high heat until thin wisps of smoke form. Add the garlic and ginger and stir constantly to infuse them into the oil until they are lightly browned, about 10 seconds, taking care not to burn them. Add the onion and Broccolini and cook, stirring frequently (stir-frying), for about 45 seconds, until slightly charred but retaining a firm texture. Add the rice cakes and stir-fry for about 45 seconds, until slightly charred, then add the brisket and sauce and stir-fry, being careful not to break the beef up, until the sauce comes to a boil, about 45 seconds. Remove from the heat and serve immediately.

NOTE:

Wok hei (aka dragon's breath) is a flavor really only attainable with an appropriate wok setup, and unfortunately, it won't really develop in a stovetop wok at home unless you have access to an outdoor, propane-powered wok. You need a fire source that hits at least 80,000 BTUs (commercial wok burners are gas-powered and can go up to 180,000 BTUs), and the heat must be able to travel up around the sides of the wok (an obvious danger in the home kitchen). The high heat sears food without overcooking it, leaving vegetables vibrant and meat succulent, but more importantly, the char-like flavor imparted when vaporized water and fats (sent airborne when the pan is shaken in such a way to toss the contents of the wok into the air) interact with that high heat shooting up from the wok burner is distinct to high-heat wok cooking. But don't worry, if you don't have this sort of setup at home, you can still make a great stir-fry in a home; the dragon's breath will simply be less prevalent.

Salt and Pepper Chicken-Fried Steak

SERVES 2 AS A MAIN COURSE

This is a beefy take on the Chinese staple of salt and pepper calamari, wherein the squid is fried with a deliciously light, crispy batter, then tossed among flavorful aromatics like green onions, garlic, jalapeños, and shallots. For me, the fried bits of crust and vegetables are the star of the show—a burst of flavor best enjoyed over a canvas of Fundamental Steamed Rice (page 87) and Chinese Sausage and Fresh Field Peas Salad (shown here and on page 117).

Cube steak, often used for Southern chicken-fried steak, is a beef round beaten with a mallet to break up its tough, fibrous muscle. You can also beat a thin slice ¼ inch (6 mm) of top or bottom round with the pointy side of a meat mallet yourself. It's a great way to relieve stress!

1 cup (240 ml) buttermilk

FOR THE DREDGE:

1 tablespoon Chinese five-spice powder

1 teaspoon salt, plus more as needed

1 teaspoon ground white pepper, plus more as needed (see Note)

1 cup (120 g) all-purpose flour

2 tablespoons cornstarch

8 ounces (225 g) cube steak, pounded ¼ inch (6 mm) thick and cut into thin oval-shaped pieces of steak, about 1½ by 3½ inches (4 cm by 9 cm)

½ cup (120 ml) canola oil

6 green onions, green and white parts cut into thin rounds (about ¼ cup / 25 g)

½ medium jalapeño chile, cut into thin rounds

2 cloves garlic, thinly sliced

1 shallot, peeled and halved lengthwise, then thinly sliced

Pour the buttermilk into a medium to large bowl and set aside.

MAKE THE DREDGE: In a small skillet over medium heat, toast the Chinese five-spice powder for 30 seconds, or until fragrant. Allow to cool, then place in a bowl with the salt, white pepper, flour, and cornstarch and mix thoroughly, then pour onto a baking sheet.

Thoroughly dust the steak in the dredge. Dip each cube into the buttermilk, then dredge again to thoroughly coat each piece of beef and set aside on a plate.

In a 10-inch (25 cm) cast-iron skillet, heat the canola oil over medium-high heat. Working in batches as necessary, add just a few pieces of beef at a time to avoid overcrowding the pan and dropping the oil temperature. Fry until golden brown, flipping after 2 to 3 minutes to brown each side.

Transfer the beef to a plate and discard all but 1 tablespoon of the oil left in the pan. Add the green onions, jalapeño, garlic, and shallot to the pan and cook, stirring constantly, for about 10 seconds. Return the steak to the pan and stir to combine, gently coating the steak with the aromatics.

Remove from the heat, season with additional salt and white pepper if needed, and serve immediately.

NOTE:

Many Chinese recipes call for white pepper, which is spicier and more pungent than floral black pepper. It's also favored in fine dining restaurants, as it leaves a cleaner look in lighter colored dishes.

Pot Roast with Daikon and Shiitake Mushrooms

SERVES 4 TO 6 AS A MAIN COURSE

Though pot roast is historically associated with European settlers in New England, I had my fair share growing up in Atlanta. I was especially fascinated with the rich, brown gravy, which my mom made even better with soy sauce and Maggi seasoning (see Note), an umami upgrade unique to our household. The shiitake mushrooms add depth of flavor to the dish, while the daikon is a light, crisp alternative to the usual potatoes. Serve on top Fundamental Steamed Rice (page 87) to soak up all that great gravy.

2 tablespoons canola oil

1 boneless beef chuck pot roast (3 to 3½ pounds / 1.4 to 1.6 kg), trimmed

Salt and black pepper

2 tablespoons unsalted butter

2 medium shallots, peeled and halved

1-inch (2.5 cm) piece fresh ginger, peeled and cut into ¼-inch (6 mm) pieces

4 cloves garlic, halved

1 large carrot, peeled and cut into 1-inch (2.5 cm) pieces

5 ounces (140 g) shiitake mushrooms, stems removed and caps cut into 1-inch (2.5 cm) pieces

1 tablespoon tomato paste

4½ teaspoons all-purpose flour

2 cups (480 ml) Chicken Stock (page 189), or store-bought low-sodium chicken or beef stock

1 tablespoon soy sauce

1 teaspoon Maggi seasoning (see Note)

2 sprigs thyme

½ medium daikon, peeled and cut into 1-inch (2.5 cm) pieces (1½ cups / 180 g), reserved in water

In a large Dutch oven, heat the oil over medium-high heat and season the chuck roast with salt and black pepper. When thin wisps of smoke form, place the beef in the Dutch oven and brown on all sides, 5 to 6 minutes total. Remove the roast from the pot and set aside, then add the butter, shallots, ginger, garlic, carrots, and mushrooms and season with salt and black pepper. Cook, stirring occasionally, until the carrots are vibrant in color and starting to soften, 3 to 4 minutes. Stir in the tomato paste and flour and cook for another minute, then add the stock, soy sauce, Maggi, and thyme and stir well to combine.

Bring to a boil, then reduce the heat to maintain a simmer and return the beef to the Dutch oven. Loosely cover the pot and braise until nearly fork-tender, about 2½ hours. Carefully flip the pot roast, add the daikon, and continue to braise, partially covered, until the beef is fork tender, about 30 minutes. Let cool slightly, then serve. Refrigerate leftovers in an airtight container with any leftover liquid for up to 3 days.

NOTE:

Maggi seasoning is a sauce used widely in Asia (but invented in Switzerland in the late 1800s) made from hydrolyzed wheat proteins that ups a dish's umami content with sumptuous flavors of roasted meats.

Braised Short Ribs with Onion Marmalade

SERVES 4 AS A MAIN COURSE

Short ribs are my favorite cut of beef, not just for their rich beef flavor, but for their versatility. They can be grilled without adornment, pounded thin before being marinated and grilled Korean-style, or simply thrown in the oven to roast. In this one-pot recipe, we cook down sweet Vidalia onions, native to an area that is a few hours southeast of Atlanta on the way to Savannah, before adding flavorful friends like ginger, star anise, and sorghum syrup. If you can't find Vidalia onions, use standard yellow onions. When serving, let the meat and resulting sauce be the star, simply ladled over roasted or mashed potatoes.

4 (4-ounce / 115 g) pieces boneless beef chuck short ribs, or boneless beef chuck flap

Salt and black pepper

2 tablespoons canola oil, plus more as needed

4 cloves garlic, crushed

1-inch (2.5 cm) piece fresh ginger, peeled and cut in half

3 Vidalia onions, thinly sliced (2 to 2½ cups / 680 g)

2 cups (480 ml) Chicken Stock (page 189)

2 tablespoons soy sauce

2 tablespoons sorghum syrup

2 tablespoons apple cider vinegar

2 star anise pods

Season the short ribs all over with salt and black pepper. In a large Dutch oven, heat the oil over medium-high heat until thin wisps of smoke appear. Carefully place the short ribs in the pan and brown each side, 1 to 2 minutes per side. Set the seared beef aside on a plate.

If necessary, add more oil so the bottom of the pan is thinly coated with oil. Add the garlic and ginger and stir constantly to infuse them into the oil for 20 to 30 seconds, taking care not to burn them. Add the onions, reduce the heat to medium-low, and cook, stirring occasionally, until they have cooked down to roughly one-third of the volume, 8 to 10 minutes (a little bit of color on the onions is OK).

Add the stock, soy sauce, sorghum syrup, vinegar, and star anise pods to the pot, stir well, scraping the bottom of the pot, and nestle the short ribs into the liquid. Loosely cover the pot, reduce the heat to maintain a slow simmer, and cook until fork-tender, about 3 hours, replenishing with water as needed to maintain the original level of the cooking liquid.

Serve immediately, though this dish can be cooled and stored in an airtight container in the fridge for up to 1 week before reheating and serving.

CHAPTER 6

Chicken

Patriarch

I wasn't close to my father growing up, not for any real reason other than the fact that my mother was such a larger-than-life character for me. But since her passing, my father and I have connected on a deeper level, and the success of Lazy Betty has given us a new foundation on which our relationship has come into bloom as fellow chefs and as father and son.

My mother was an instinctual cook, but my father was definitely the better cook of the family, more disciplined and technical, and is now my go-to source for advice on Chinese cooking. I learned only ten years ago that he was also a chef back in Malaysia before coming to Atlanta, and while my mom cooked out of necessity to survive here, my father *chose* to be a chef, bringing those skills with him here to the United States.

In this book, he is the main inspiration for the Grilled Mandarin Beef Ribs (page 159), and at one point, my family produced a chili crisp dubbed "Pappy Hsu Chili Crisp" in his honor (the Mala Oil on page 247 is a rendition of that). I guess you could say that while my mother was the larger influence on me, especially on the abstract ideas like comfort, inclusivity, and diligence, I've received a great deal from my father regarding the technical side and craft of cooking. From the techniques used to the passion for cooking, I can see a lot of him in the pages of this book.

LEFT: Pictured here is mala oil, a precursor to Pappy Hsu's Chili Crisp, which Ron's family bottles in very small batches.

OPPOSITE, CLOCKWISE FROM TOP: Ron's siblings and father; Ron's father making egg rolls at Hunan Village; Ron's mother and father.

95

Roast Chicken and Rice Casserole

SERVES 4 TO 6 AS A MAIN COURSE

This is my Southern/Asian mashup of a dish every culture has: chicken and rice. Very few things satisfy the soul more than a one-pot meal, and this one materialized out of an early, horribly failed attempt at making Hainanese chicken rice, wherein I essentially threw raw chicken and uncooked rice in a pot and hoped for the best. I ended up with a hodgepodge of tough chicken and rice that was somehow simultaneously either crunchy or mushy and devoid of flavor. Lesson learned: Respect traditional methods and cook ingredients in ways that will ensure their harmony. In this case we build flavor by slowly browning the chicken before sautéing aromatics in the resulting fats, only then adding the rice before nestling the chicken on top to slowly and symbiotically cook as one. Thankfully I figured that out, and this dish is now one of my family's favorite meals.

1 tablespoon canola oil

4 chicken leg quarters, split into drumsticks and thighs (about 2½ pounds / 1.2 kg)

Salt and white pepper

½ cup (80 g) finely chopped onion

3 cloves garlic, thinly sliced

1-inch (2.5 cm) piece fresh ginger, peeled and minced

5 ounces (140 g) shiitake mushrooms, stems removed and caps cut into ½-inch (12 mm) pieces (about 1 cup)

3 cups (555 g) jasmine rice or other long-grain rice, rinsed and drained

3½ cups (840 ml) Chicken Stock (page 189)

1 can (13½ ounces / 405 ml) unsweetened coconut milk

2 stalks lemongrass, top half removed and discarded, bottom half split lengthwise and crushed with the side of a chef's knife

¼ cup (15 g) chopped cilantro

2 green onions, green parts only, thinly sliced

1 lime, cut into 6 wedges

Preheat the oven to 425°F (220°C).

In a 9 by 13-inch (23 by 33 cm) metal roasting pan or 5-quart (4.7 L) Dutch oven, heat the oil over medium heat. Season the chicken with salt and white pepper, then place the chicken in the pan and sear for 3 minutes. Transfer the pan to the oven and roast until golden brown, about 5 minutes, then flip the chicken and roast for an additional 5 minutes. Remove the chicken from the oven and transfer to a plate.

Discard any excess oil (more than 1 tablespoon) from the pan and place it over medium heat. Add the onion, garlic, and ginger and cook, stirring frequently, until the onion becomes translucent but does not brown, 3 to 4 minutes. Add the mushrooms and continue to cook until softened, another 3 to 4 minutes, then add the rice, chicken stock, and coconut milk. Season with salt and white pepper and stir to combine.

Nestle the chicken and lemongrass on top of the rice and increase the heat to high to bring the liquid to a boil. Cover the pan with aluminum foil or a lid, place in the oven, and bake until the rice is tender and the chicken is cooked through, about 15 minutes.

Remove the pan from the oven and allow the dish to rest, covered, on the stovetop for an additional 10 minutes. Garnish with the cilantro and green onions and serve immediately, right in the pan, with the lime wedges.

Soy-Braised Chicken

SERVES 2 TO 4 AS A MAIN COURSE

This simple, succulent dish rich with aromatic ginger and star anise is a commonly served dish in Chinese households, and mine was no exception; however, I really love the crispy variation (see Note). Cook low and slow for tender chicken, and reuse the cooking liquid up to three times, replenishing the water lost in cooking as needed. It will get more flavorful each time, so much so that it could even be used as a broth for noodle soup. Serve this chicken with Stir-Fried Collard Greens with Bacon (page 51) and Sriracha-Spiced Baked Mac and Cheese with Panko Crust (page 224) for an Asian-influenced Southern meal.

1½ cups (360 ml) soy sauce

2 tablespoons bourbon

½ cup (120 ml) sorghum syrup

3 star anise pods

1 cinnamon stick

1-inch (2.5 cm) piece fresh ginger, peeled and sliced ¼ inch (6 mm) thick

2 green onions, green and white parts, cut into 1-inch (2.5 cm) pieces

1 teaspoon white peppercorns

4 chicken leg quarters (about 2½ pounds / 1.2 kg)

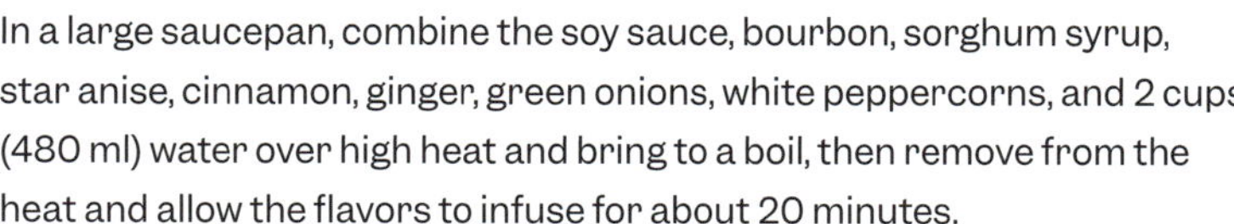

In a large saucepan, combine the soy sauce, bourbon, sorghum syrup, star anise, cinnamon, ginger, green onions, white peppercorns, and 2 cups (480 ml) water over high heat and bring to a boil, then remove from the heat and allow the flavors to infuse for about 20 minutes.

Add the chicken legs to the pot and place over low heat. Once a low simmer is reached, adjust the heat to maintain a low simmer (be sure the simmer is low to ensure tender chicken) and cook for 25 minutes, then flip the chicken legs and cook for another 25 minutes. Remove from the heat and allow the chicken to cool down in the liquid until you are ready to eat it (at least 10 minutes and up to 30 minutes) to let the cooking finish and flavors penetrate the chicken (if necessary, reheat the chicken by bringing the liquid to a simmer over low heat and cooking for about 5 minutes).

When ready to serve, use a heavy cleaver to slice the chicken through the bone and serve. Strain, cool, and refrigerate the cooking liquid in an airtight container for up 1 week to use up to two more times.

NOTE:

For deliciously crispy skin, lay the chicken, skin side up, on a baking sheet after it is done cooking. Refrigerate uncovered overnight. When ready to proceed, in a large, heavy pot set up with an oil thermometer, heat 4 inches (10 cm) vegetable oil over high heat to 350°F (175°C) when measured with an oil thermometer. Have a spider ready. When the oil is hot, add the chicken to the oil and fry it until the chicken is heated through and its skin is crispy, 3 to 5 minutes. Serve immediately.

Chicken Stock

MAKES 2½ TO 3 QUARTS (2.4 TO 2.8 L)

Chicken stock was one of the first things I ever learned to make in the early days at my mother's restaurant, Hunan Village. Every morning, we'd open the kitchen and cover nothing more than chicken necks and backs with water in a 35-gallon (133 L) vessel, keeping the stocks clean and simple with no aromatics or browning of the bones. The pot would simmer constantly throughout the day, replenished with water as we used it as the base for all our soups and in our stir-fries.

Later, after culinary school, I came back beaming and brimming with my newfound schoolboy knowledge (or so I thought), introducing mirepoix and lightly browned bones to our stock one day. A long-time server and all-around utility man known as "Uncle Raymond" (despite no blood relation) was appalled to see the difference in color and flavor of the stock, quickly reprimanding me that "this is not a Chinese stock!" Without knowing it, Uncle Raymond had taught me one of the most valuable lessons a young cook could learn: School was but a single source of knowledge, and not the ultimate authority. What I learned there needed to be tempered with a respect for the origins of the Chinese food I grew up eating. Ultimately, the clean, pure taste of unroasted bones and the aromatic addition of mirepoix won out in my stocks, but the exchange made me realize that combining different cuisines must be done with care.

3 pounds (1.4 kg) chicken bones, necks, and backs

1½ pounds (680 g) chicken feet

2 green onions, quartered

3 cloves garlic, crushed with the side of a chef's knife

1-inch (2.5 cm) piece fresh ginger, crushed with the side of a chef's knife

½ large yellow onion, chopped

2 star anise pods

1 teaspoon whole white peppercorns

In a stockpot, combine all of the ingredients with 3 quarts (2.8 L) water and bring to a boil over medium-high heat. Reduce the heat to maintain a low simmer. Noting the volume of liquid in the pot, cook for 4 to 6 hours, skimming any sediment and fat that rises to the top every hour or so, replenishing the liquid to the original volume with water as needed.

Remove from the heat, allow to cool slightly, then strain through a sieve. Discard the solids and allow the liquid to fully cool. Remove any solidified chicken fat from the top of the cooled stock and save for another purpose, such as Hainanese Chicken Rice Rice (page 68), by refrigerating it for up to 2 weeks. Store the stock refrigerated in an airtight container for up to 1 week or frozen for up to 3 months.

Curried Chicken Salad with Asian Pear

SERVES 2 TO 4 AS A MAIN COURSE

Fresh Asian pear adds a crunchy sweetness that works in harmony with the curry powder in this version of a classic chicken salad, perfect for summer picnics. Asian pears can be found in many grocery stores, especially Asian markets (they are often wrapped individually in a foam netting), but crisp apples can be used as well. Eat this salad with a crisp piece of lettuce tucked inside a soft grocery store croissant—just like the ones my grandma used to get me at the DeKalb Farmers Market, where she worked when I was growing up.

1 pound (455 g) boneless, skinless chicken breasts (about 3 medium)

Salt and white pepper

¼ cup (60 ml) mayonnaise (preferably Duke's)

Juice of ½ lime (about 1 tablespoon)

1 tablespoon Madras curry powder

2 tablespoons chopped celery

1 tablespoon chopped red onion

25 mint leaves, chopped

½ cup (75 g) chopped Asian pear

In a medium saucepan, place the chicken in a single layer and cover with water. Season the water with salt and white pepper and bring to a simmer over medium heat, then reduce the heat to maintain a simmer and cook until the chicken is cooked through, 8 to 10 minutes. Remove the chicken from the liquid and allow it to cool, discarding the liquid.

Meanwhile, place the mayonnaise, lime juice, curry powder, and salt and white pepper to taste in a large bowl and stir to combine. Add the celery, onion, mint, and pear to the bowl. When the chicken is cooled, shred it and add to the bowl. Gently mix to combine and serve immediately, or chill covered in the refrigerator for up to 1 day.

Taiwanese Chicken Nuggets

SERVES 2 TO 4 AS AN APPETIZER

Growing up, I liked homemade Taiwanese chicken just fine, but this isn't a time-honored family recipe. It wasn't until I incorporated the influence of Chick-fil-A, always a steady presence in my Southern life from the early days, that this chicken became one of my favorite Taiwanese dishes. Once I discovered their chicken nuggets, I immediately started to compare them to what we were making at my mom's restaurant. This led me to incorporate tangy buttermilk into our brine, adding an acidic, viscous element that absorbed more of the dredge, making for more crunch, and upping the addictive nature of the distinct Taiwanese flavorings—perfect with a side of honey for dipping.

6 skinless, boneless chicken thighs (1½ pounds / 680 g), cut into ½-inch (12 mm) pieces

½ cup (120 ml) buttermilk

1 large egg

FOR THE DREDGE:

2 cups (255 g) cornstarch

2 tablespoons Chinese five-spice powder

FOR THE SEASONING:

2 teaspoons salt

2 teaspoons sugar

1 teaspoon ground ginger

½ teaspoon ground cayenne pepper

½ teaspoon ground Szechuan pepper

Canola oil, for deep-frying

20 basil leaves

Red Pepper Marmalade (page 243) and honey, for dipping (optional)

In a large, nonreactive bowl, combine the chicken and the buttermilk. Brine for at least 30 minutes or up to 4 hours (refrigerate if marinating longer than 30 minutes, and remove the mixture from the refrigerator roughly 30 minutes before you are ready to proceed).

MEANWHILE, MAKE THE DREDGE: In a medium bowl, thoroughly combine the cornstarch and Chinese five-spice powder and set aside.

MAKE THE SEASONING: In a small bowl, thoroughly combine the salt, sugar, ground ginger, cayenne, and Szechuan pepper and set aside.

When ready to proceed, drain the buttermilk from the chicken in a colander, discard the buttermilk, and return the chicken to the bowl. Beat the egg in a small bowl, add it to the chicken, and mix thoroughly. Add the dredge to the chicken and mix to thoroughly coat. Shake off any excess dredge through a sieve and return the chicken to the bowl to prepare for frying.

Set up a frying station. In a large, heavy pot set up with an oil thermometer, heat 2 inches (5 cm) oil over high heat to 375°F (190°C). Have a spider and large bowl ready. When the oil is hot, add the chicken to the oil. Work in batches as necessary, adding just a few pieces of chicken at a time to avoid overcrowding the oil and dropping the oil temperature. Fry until light golden brown, about 4 minutes, occasionally breaking up any clumps using the spider. Add the basil leaves and fry for another 20 seconds.

Use the spider to transfer the chicken and basil from the pot to the clean bowl, shaking off excess oil, and sprinkle with the seasoning mixture to taste. Serve right away with a side of red pepper marmalade and honey if desired.

Buttermilk Fried Chicken

SERVES 4 AS A MAIN COURSE

Fried chicken is probably the South's most iconic dish, but so many other cuisines fry birds just as well. Think Japanese karaage, KFC (Korean fried chicken), Austrian chicken schnitzel, or even the chicken Parmesan of America's Italian diaspora. This recipe is an homage to my mom's Asian-style version of the Southern classic, loading the Southern buttermilk brine with aromatics and adding crunch-boosting cornstarch to the dredge before deep-frying in a big, heavy pot rather than the shallow fry of the usual cast-iron pan. I stay in line with my Chinese upbringing by eating this crispy fried bird with a bowl of Fundamental Steamed Rice (page 87), simple smashed cucumbers, and stir-fried cabbage, but it would also go well with more Southern-style sides, such as mac and cheese, Stir-Fried Collard Greens with Bacon (page 51), or Asian Pear and Napa Cabbage Slaw (see page 52), with plenty of hot sauce on the side. And if you're looking for a high-octane upgrade, drizzle the freshly fried, hot, crackly chicken with a few heavy spoonfuls of chili crisp and a good drizzle of honey. Just when you thought fried chicken couldn't get better, the sweet heat and flavor boost will send you over the moon!

FOR THE BRINE:

4 cups (960 ml) buttermilk

1 teaspoon ground dried thyme

1 teaspoon ground black pepper

1 teaspoon ground cayenne pepper

1 teaspoon ground celery seed

1 teaspoon ground coriander

1 teaspoon ground cumin

4 cloves garlic, crushed with the side of a chef's knife

1 teaspoon salt

4 chicken leg quarters (about 2½ pounds / 1.2 kg)

FOR THE DREDGE:

2 cups (255 g) cornstarch

2 cups (240 g) all-purpose flour

1 teaspoon dried thyme

1 teaspoon ground black pepper

1 teaspoon ground cayenne pepper

1 teaspoon ground celery seed

1 teaspoon ground coriander

1 teaspoon ground cumin

½ teaspoon garlic powder

½ teaspoon onion powder

1 teaspoon salt

1 teaspoon white pepper

Canola oil, for deep-frying

Salt

MAKE THE BRINE: Place the buttermilk, dried thyme, black pepper, cayenne pepper, celery seed, coriander, cumin, garlic, and salt in a large nonreactive bowl and mix well to combine. Add the chicken to the brine and refrigerate for at least 2 hours or up to 8 hours. Remove the chicken from the refrigerator roughly 1 hour before you are ready to proceed.

MEANWHILE, MAKE THE DREDGE: Place the cornstarch, flour, dried thyme, black pepper, cayenne pepper, celery seed, coriander, cumin, garlic powder, onion powder, salt, and white pepper in a large bowl and mix well to combine.

Working one leg at a time, remove the chicken from the brine, gently shaking off some of the excess liquid but leaving some to help the dredge adhere to the chicken. Place the chicken into the dredge and coat, mixing the chicken and dredge with your hands and firmly pressing so the dredge adheres to the chicken. Place the dredged chicken on a tray and set aside. Repeat with the remaining chicken.

When all of the chicken is dredged, set up a frying station. In a large, heavy pot set up with an oil thermometer, heat 6 inches (15 cm) vegetable oil over high heat to 325°F (165°C). Have a spider and large bowl ready. When the oil is hot, add the chicken to the oil. Work in batches as necessary, adding just a few pieces of chicken at a time to avoid overcrowding the oil and dropping the oil temperature. Fry until dark golden brown and cooked through, 15 to 20 minutes, or until a meat thermometer inserted in the thickest part of the meat reaches 165°F (75°C).

Use the spider to transfer the chicken to a large bowl, sprinkle with salt to taste, and gently toss, then transfer to a serving platter and serve immediately.

Kung Pao Chicken with Fried Peanuts

SERVES 2 AS A MAIN COURSE

This nostalgic classic of Chinese American cuisine is another example of the velveting process explained on page 163. It was obviously one of the more popular dishes at Hunan Village, but it scores extra points with me because it features one of Georgia's proudest ingredients: peanuts. If you have it in you, deep-frying the peanuts makes them incredibly fragrant, but a quick pan-toast will suffice as well. Serve with Fundamental Steamed Rice (page 87) or a bowl of creamy grits with sriracha on the side if you like more spice.

FOR THE MARINADE:

1 tablespoon oyster sauce

1 teaspoon curry powder

1 teaspoon soy sauce

1 tablespoon cornstarch

1 teaspoon crushed red pepper

12 ounces (340 g) boneless skinless chicken thighs, sliced into ½-inch (12 mm) cubes

3 tablespoons canola oil

3 Szechuan peppercorns

3 cloves garlic, thinly sliced

1-inch (2.5 cm) piece fresh ginger, peeled and cut into 1 by ⅛-inch (2.5 cm by 3 mm) matchstick strips

10 basil leaves

3 pieces okra, cut into ¼-inch (6 mm) pieces

½ red bell pepper, cut into ½-inch (12 mm) cubes

½ medium red onion, cut into ½-inch (12 mm) cubes

½ stalk celery, cut into ½-inch (12 mm) cubes

1 teaspoon curry powder

1 teaspoon oyster sauce

¼ cup (40 g) peanuts, deep-fried or pan-roasted

MAKE THE MARINADE: In a medium bowl, mix the oyster sauce, curry powder, soy sauce, cornstarch, and crushed red pepper.

Add the chicken and mix thoroughly, then cover and refrigerate for at least 30 minutes or up to 6 hours.

In a wok or large skillet, heat 2 tablespoons of the oil over medium-high heat. Add the marinated chicken and cook, frequently stirring (stir-frying), until just cooked through, 2 to 3 minutes.

Transfer the chicken to a bowl, then add the remaining 1 tablespoon oil to the pan. Add the Szechuan peppercorns, garlic, ginger, and basil and stir-fry until fragrant, 10 to 15 seconds. Add the okra, bell pepper, onion, and celery and stir-fry until tender but still crisp, about 45 seconds.

Return the chicken to the pan and add the curry powder and oyster sauce to the pan. Stir-fry for another 1½ minutes, or until the ingredients are thoroughly mixed, hot, and fragrant, then transfer to a bowl, top with the peanuts, and serve immediately.

General Tso's Chicken

SERVES 2 TO 4 AS A MAIN COURSE

My mom discovered this American Chinese restaurant classic on a trip to San Francisco to visit old restaurateur friends. Quickly adding it to her menu, it became our most popular dish, bypassing sweet and sour chicken and Mongolian beef for the title due to its use of dark meat and its hint of spice. My evolved version incorporates buttermilk powder (easily available online) to give the sweet, crunchy chicken a bit of tang while keeping the coating light and crisp.

FOR THE CHICKEN:

1 pound (455 g) boneless, skinless chicken thighs (6 to 8 thighs), cut into ½-inch (12 mm) pieces

1 large egg, beaten

1 tablespoon Shaoxing cooking wine

1 teaspoon Chinese five-spice powder

½ teaspoon salt

¾ cup (95 g) cornstarch

1 tablespoon buttermilk powder

Canola oil, for frying

FOR THE SAUCE:

1 tablespoon soy sauce

1 teaspoon toasted sesame oil

2 tablespoons ketchup

1 tablespoon sorghum syrup

½ cup (120 ml) Chicken Stock (page 189)

1 teaspoon sambal oelek, sriracha, or Tabasco sauce

1½ teaspoons cornstarch

Salt and white pepper

FOR THE STIR-FRY:

1 tablespoon canola oil

3 cloves garlic, thinly sliced

1-inch (2.5 cm) piece fresh ginger, cut into 1 by ¼-inch (2.5 cm by 6 mm) matchstick strips

1 cup (80 g) small broccoli florets

Fundamental Steamed Rice (page 87), optional

In a medium bowl, combine the chicken, egg, Shaoxing cooking wine, Chinese five-spice powder, and salt and mix thoroughly. Add the cornstarch and buttermilk powder and mix again, then set aside to marinate while you set up a frying station.

In a large, heavy pot set up with an oil thermometer, heat 2 inches (5 cm) of canola oil over high heat to 400°F (205°C). Have a spider and paper towel–lined plate ready. When the oil is hot, add the chicken to the oil. Work in batches as necessary, adding just a few pieces of chicken at a time to avoid overcrowding the oil and dropping the oil temperature. Fry until golden brown, then use the spider to transfer the chicken to the paper towel–lined plate and set aside.

MAKE THE SAUCE: Combine the soy sauce, sesame oil, ketchup, sorghum syrup, chicken stock, sambal, cornstarch, and salt and white pepper to taste in a bowl, mix well, and set aside.

MAKE THE STIR-FRY: In a large wok or skillet, heat the 1 tablespoon canola oil over medium-high heat until thin wisps of smoke form. Add the garlic and ginger and stir constantly to infuse them into the oil until they are lightly browned, about 10 seconds, taking care not to burn them.

Whisk the sauce one more time and add it and the broccoli to the pan and cook, stirring frequently (stir-frying), until the sauce thickens, about 45 seconds, then add the chicken and continue to stir-fry for another 30 seconds. Once finished, transfer to a bowl and serve with steamed rice if desired.

Chinese Barbecued Chicken

SERVES 2 TO 4 AS A MAIN COURSE

This is the kind of dish that chefs love to have on their menus: little prep, forgiving to cook, and a high payoff in terms of yield and flavor. At home, it shows the benefit of a well-stocked pantry: If you've got the Char Siu Marinade (see page 244) lying around from another day, you're simply coating the chicken with it, letting it marinate, then grilling it (which also means there's virtually no cleanup). Plus, even picky eaters like my daughter will absolutely love it.

6 chicken drumsticks (1½ pounds / 680 g)

1 cup (240 ml) Char Siu Marinade (page 244)

Place the chicken in a zip-top plastic bag and add ½ cup (120 ml) of the marinade. Seal the bag, pressing out as much air as possible and making sure the chicken is coated with the marinade. Marinate, refrigerated, for at least 4 hours or up to overnight. Remove the chicken from the refrigerator roughly 1 hour before you are ready to proceed.

Preheat your clean and seasoned grill over medium-low heat (see Note).

Remove the chicken from the marinade, discard the bag and the used marinade, and place the chicken on the hot grill. Cook, turning and basting with the remaining ½ cup (120 ml) marinade every 2 minutes, until the juices run clear when the chicken is pierced with the tip of a knife. Serve immediately.

NOTE:

Be sure to use a lower heat on the grill to avoid burning the sugars in the marinade before the chicken cooks through. Also, my late mother taught me to use 3 to 4 green onion roots to brush lacquers, marinades, and sauces onto grilled items; this adds flavor and aroma while avoiding the melting of synthetic brush bristles. Throwing the green onions on to the grill for about 2 minutes per side is also a bonus snack if you wanted to add some green to this dish.

CHAPTER 7

Noodles, Dumplings, and More

Dumpling Making

Making dumplings is a huge part of my life and identity. Some families teach their kids to ride a bike, others how to throw a baseball. I spent half of every Saturday while growing up making dumplings with the employees of our restaurant, cousins, aunts, and uncles. It was a pastime for us, and to be honest, I really didn't look forward to it at all. But eventually, I learned to love it and the valuable lessons standing around a table with others making dumplings taught me.

Like the value of teamwork. Cliché perhaps, but when I saw every person making those dumplings, from dishwasher to cook to boss, I saw that every person in a restaurant (and in the world, for that matter) has an important, necessary role, playing a part in creating something greater the sum of its parts. Not to

mention camaraderie. I became friends with these people, learning their histories, the path to Hunan Village. I learned of their plights as they worked long hours to send money back home to their families. I also learned several other languages—mainly kitchen talk, with a major in profanity. Most importantly, I learned the value of connection, which I stress at Lazy Betty today. We don't just sling food and drinks; we try to connect with each other, and we try to connect with the guests in our dining room. Great food is simply the medium to do so.

Fast-forward twenty-five years (and who knows how many dumplings) from those early sessions, and I'm keeping it in the family, teaching my daughter the tradition of dumpling making. As we fold dough over fillings together, those fillings might change, adapt, and evolve, but the lessons of connection and togetherness do not.

OPPOSITE: Jackie, Calliope, and Ron making dumplings.

ABOVE, CLOCKWISE FROM TOP LEFT: Calliope kneading the dough; Ron portioning the dough pieces before they are rolled flat and filled; finished dumplings with pleats.

Ron's Le Bernardin Family Meal: Penne Pasta with Pulled Pork and Broccolini

SERVES 3 TO 4 AS A MAIN COURSE

This was one of my go-to family meals when I was the poissonnier (fish cook) at Le Bernardin, so it works well whenever one has to cook for sixty hungry chefs in one of the world's great restaurants. Don't worry, though, it's a great dish for them or a family, satisfying with tender, richly flavored pork, braising liquid–soaked pasta, and crunchy Broccolini. Or simply cut it in half for a date night for two.

FOR THE PULLED PORK:

1 tablespoon canola oil

2 pounds (910 g) boneless pork butt

Salt and black pepper

½ medium onion, chopped (about ½ cup / 80 g)

3 cloves garlic, minced

1-inch (2.5 cm) piece fresh ginger, peeled and cut into 1 by ¼-inch (2.5 cm by 6 mm) matchstick strips

½ cup (120 ml) hoisin sauce

2 cups (480 ml) Chicken Stock (page 189)

¼ cup (60 ml) apple cider vinegar

2 tablespoons fish sauce

1 teaspoon soy sauce

1 teaspoon toasted sesame oil

2 star anise pods

2 cups (7 ounces/200 g) dried penne pasta

5 ounces (140 g) Broccolini, cut into 1-inch (2.5 cm) pieces (about 1½ cups)

1 tablespoon toasted sesame seeds

MAKE THE PULLED PORK: In a Dutch oven, heat the canola oil over medium heat. Season the pork with salt and black pepper on all sides, then place it in the pot and brown all over, about 2 minutes per side. Remove the pork from the pot and set aside.

Add the onion, garlic, and ginger to the pot and cook, stirring occasionally and without too much browning, for 2 to 3 minutes. Stir in the hoisin sauce and cook for 2 more minutes, stirring occasionally. Add the stock, vinegar, fish sauce, soy sauce, sesame oil, and star anise to the pot and bring to a simmer. Reduce the heat to maintain a simmer, loosely cover, and cook until the pork is fork tender, 3 to 4 hours.

When the pork is cooked, remove it from the pot and place it in a large bowl or baking dish and gently shred using two large forks. Discard the star anise pods. Return the pork and any accumulated juices to the braising liquid in the pot.

Bring a large pot of salted water to a boil, then cook the pasta as directed on the box. When the pasta is about 90 seconds away from al dente doneness, add the Broccolini to the boiling water.

When the pasta is al dente, reserve 1 cup (240 ml) of the cooking water, then strain the pasta and Broccolini and add them to the pot of pulled pork. Stir to combine, adjusting the consistency of the dish with the reserved pasta water as needed. Serve immediately, garnishing with the sesame seeds. Store leftovers in an airtight container for up to 2 days

Pimiento Cheese Wontons

MAKES 10 WONTONS; SERVES 4 AS AN APPETIZER

The traditional Southern spread meets the classic Chinese wonton, offering far more action than the standard crab Rangoon. My siblings Howard and Anita serve a version of this at their restaurant Sweet Auburn BBQ, but they serve it with sweet, Thai-style chili sauce, whereas I like it with the Southern-style Red Pepper Marmalade (page 243). To make the pimiento cheese filling, I use sriracha rather than the usual Tabasco sauce for a more subtle tart vinegar profile. The filling also works great on its own as a pimiento cheese dip—simply increase the mayonnaise or buttermilk as desired to make it more spreadable.

1 recipe pimiento cheese from Pimiento Cheese with Scallion Pancakes (page 211), chilled

Cornstarch, for dusting

10 square wonton skins

Canola oil, for frying

Red Pepper Marmalade (page 243) or Sriracha Ranch (page 84), for serving

Place the pimiento cheese in a small bowl, dust a baking sheet with cornstarch, open your wonton package, and fill a small bowl with water.

Place 1 wonton wrapper in your hand, then place roughly 1 tablespoon of the pimiento cheese in the center of the wrapper. Wet the tip of your index finger and moisten the outer edge of the wrapper. Fold each corner of the wrapper up so that each point meets to form a pyramid. Pinch the edges of the dough from the point of the pyramid down to the base to seal the wonton while squeezing out any excess air inside. Set the completed wontons on the prepared baking sheet and repeat until all the wontons are wrapped

When all the wontons are wrapped, set up a frying station. In a large, heavy pot set up with an oil thermometer, heat 2 inches (5 cm) of canola oil over high heat to 350°F (175°C). Have a spider and paper towel–lined plate ready. When the oil is hot, add the wontons to the oil and fry until golden brown and heated through, 4 to 6 minutes. Work in batches if necessary to avoid crowding and dropping the oil temperature. Use the spider to transfer the wontons to the paper towel–lined plate. When all the wontons are cooked, transfer to a serving platter and serve immediately with the red pepper marmalade or sriracha ranch.

Raw wontons can be frozen on a baking sheet in a single layer, then transferred to a zip-top plastic bag and frozen for up to 3 months, then fried from a frozen state, adding a couple of minutes to the total fry time as needed.

Pimiento Cheese with Scallion Pancakes

SERVES 4 TO 6 AS AN APPETIZER

Saturdays were for dumpling-making at my mom's restaurant, Hunan Village. But we also made plenty of wraps for moo shu from the same dough, as well as these delicious scallion pancakes, rich with sesame oil and green onions in layers created by the mini-laminating process described below. They were a favorite after-school snack for me, so as an adult, serving them with a traditional Southern pimiento cheese was a no brainer. In my version of pimiento cheese, we use flavorful sriracha rather than the usual Tabasco sauce, and we char red peppers and jalapeños on the stovetop rather than using a canned product (if push comes to shove, you'll still get good results with canned peppers). Feel free to adjust the mayonnaise or buttermilk as desired to make the dip more spreadable. Note that the scallion pancakes are best eaten fresh just after cooking, as they quickly grow hard. And if you want to diversify your caviar game, replace the usual blinis with these scallion pancakes for a warm, crisp delivery vessel.

FOR THE PIMIENTO CHEESE (MAKES ABOUT 2½ CUPS / 550 G):

1 red bell pepper

2 jalapeños

8 ounces (225 g) sharp cheddar cheese, shredded (about 2 cups)

3 ounces (85 g) cream cheese (about ⅓ cup)

⅓ cup (75 ml) mayonnaise (preferably Duke's)

1½ teaspoons Dijon mustard

1½ teaspoons sriracha

1 tablespoon Worcestershire sauce

1 tablespoon apple cider vinegar

2 tablespoons minced parsley

ingredients continue

MAKE THE PIMIENTO CHEESE: Place the red pepper and jalapeños directly on your stovetop burner grates or on a wire rack placed on the burners. Turn the flame to medium and cook until the peppers are completely blackened all over, rotating from time to time, about 4 minutes.

Alternatively, if you don't have a gas stovetop, preheat the broiler and line a baking sheet with foil. Cut the red pepper and jalapeños lengthwise in half; remove and discard the stems and seeds. Arrange the peppers, cut side down, on the prepared broiling pan and place the pan in the broiler, 5 to 6 inches from the heat source. Broil until the skin of the peppers is charred and blistered, 8 to 10 minutes.

Place the charred peppers in a bowl and cover tightly with plastic wrap to steam as they cool down, 15 to 20 minutes. When cool enough to handle, peel off the skin and discard (if using the stovetop method, remove the stems and seeds and discard as well). Finely chop the peppers and place in a food processor, add the cheddar cheese, cream cheese, mayonnaise, mustard, sriracha, Worcestershire sauce, vinegar, and parsley and pulse to combine until a nearly smooth consistency is reached. Refrigerate until fully chilled, about 1 hour.

recipe continues

FOR THE PANCAKES:

2 cups (240 g) all-purpose flour

Salt

¾ cup (180 ml) boiling water, plus more as needed

2 tablespoons toasted sesame oil

1 cup thinly sliced green onions (8 medium), white and green parts

Canola oil, for frying

MAKE THE PANCAKES: Place the flour and a pinch of salt in a large bowl. Add ¼ cup (60 ml) of the boiling water and stir with a wooden spoon to incorporate (see Note on boiling water for doughs, page 223). The dough will look shaggy and dry. Stir another ¼ cup (60 ml) boiling water into the flour. The dough will be a bit less dry, but still shaggy. Add another ¼ cup (60 ml) boiling water into the flour and mix well. At this point, the dough should form a smooth ball, and should feel tacky, but not sticky. You shouldn't need more than ¾ cup (180 ml) of the boiling water, but if the dough still feels dry, add an additional 1 tablespoon boiling water at a time until the dough comes together as described. Once the dough is cool enough to touch, knead by hand until smooth, 3 to 5 minutes. Place the dough in a bowl, cover with plastic wrap, and set aside at room temperature for 30 minutes.

To shape the pancakes, divide the dough into 10 to 12 balls just larger than Ping-Pong balls (about 1.5 ounces / 40 g each), then flatten each one with your palm. Use a rolling pin to roll each piece of dough to a disk roughly ¼ inch (6 mm) thick and 3½ inches (9 cm) in diameter, dusting with flour as necessary if the dough starts sticking. Brush each disk with a thin layer of sesame oil, sprinkle with additional salt, and evenly sprinkle the green onions across the pancakes. Roll each pancake into a log, pinching the ends to seal, then coil each log into itself to resemble a cinnamon roll. Flatten with your palm and dust both sides with flour, then roll each pancake to a ¼-inch (6 mm) thick, 3½-inch (9 cm) wide disk again.

When all the pancakes are formed, heat 1 tablespoon canola oil in a 9- or 10-inch skillet over medium heat. Place 1 pancake in the pan and cook until browned, about 1 minute. Flip and repeat. Transfer the pancake to a plate, wipe out the skillet with a paper towel, and repeat this process until all the pancakes are cooked.

Cut each pancake into quarters and serve with the pimiento cheese.

NOTE:

This book's style guide calls for the term *green onions* to be used rather than *scallions*, but "green onion pancakes" just didn't sound right as a recipe title. So, we decided to go with the traditional, recognizable name "scallion pancakes." But rest assured, these are two names for the same ingredient!

Lemon Pepper Ramen with Shredded Chicken

SERVES 2 AS A MAIN COURSE

This dish is perfect for a busy family—especially one with a noodle and broth–loving kid like mine. The ever-versatile store-bought rotisserie chicken is quickly broken down for one dinner, the leftover meat becoming an easy add-in for a subsequent meal as the bones turn chicken stock into a fortified ramen broth. All the better if you can find a lemon pepper chicken (such an iconic Southern flavor profile). Spice this ramen up by serving Mala Oil (page 247) on the side, and if you don't have chicken stock on hand to start with, use water. It will not be as rich and full, but it will still work, and be sure to add that lemon peel only at the end as instructed for maximum aromatic potency.

1 store-bought rotisserie chicken, preferably lemon-pepper flavor

FOR THE BROTH:

1½ tablespoons black peppercorns, crushed and toasted

1½ teaspoons white peppercorns, crushed and toasted

6 sprigs thyme

3 cloves garlic, crushed with the side of a chef's knife

2-inch (5 cm) piece fresh ginger, crushed with the side of a chef's knife

3 green onions, roots trimmed

2 quarts (2 L) Chicken Stock (page 189) or water

Peel of 2 lemons (no pith)

1 teaspoon fish sauce

1 teaspoon toasted sesame oil

Salt and black pepper

2 packages (3 ounces / 85 g each) dried instant ramen (reserve seasoning packets for another use)

2 large heads bok choy, halved lengthwise

1 tablespoon lemon juice (about ½ lemon)

2 large eggs, soft-boiled (see Note), peeled and halved

2 green onions, green parts only, thinly sliced

Chili crisp (optional)

recipe continues

Separate all of the chicken meat from bones. Shred 6 ounces (170 g) of the meat and set aside, reserving the remaining meat for another use. Place the bones in a large saucepan.

MAKE THE BROTH: Add the black peppercorns, white peppercorns, thyme, garlic, ginger, green onions, and chicken stock to the pot with the bones and bring to a boil over high heat. Reduce the heat to maintain a low simmer. Noting the volume of liquid in the pot, cook for 4 hours, skimming any sediment and fat that rises to the top every hour or so, replenishing the liquid to the original volume with water as needed. Add the lemon peel and simmer for an additional 15 to 20 minutes.

Remove from the heat, allow to cool slightly, then strain through a sieve, discarding the solids. Add the fish sauce and sesame oil, season with salt and black pepper, and stir to combine.

Pour 6 cups (1.4 L) of the broth (reserve the remaining broth for another use) into a large saucepan and bring to a boil over high heat. Add the noodles and bok choy and cook until the noodles are al dente, about 2 minutes. Remove the bok choy from the pot and set aside. Divide the noodles between two large ramen bowls and ladle half of the broth over each mound of noodles.

Drizzle the lemon juice over each bowl and divide the reserved bok choy, chicken, eggs, and green onions between the 2 bowls and serve immediately with chili crisp, if using.

NOTE:

To make soft-boiled eggs, place eggs in a small saucepan and cover with water. Bring to a boil over high heat, then cook for 5 minutes. Remove the pan from the heat and place under cold running water until eggs are cool enough to handle, then peel and halve for use in the recipe.

Vermicelli Noodle Salad with Taiwanese Buttermilk Fried Chicken Nuggets

SERVES 2 AS A MAIN COURSE

This was a crowd favorite (and mine) at a former Vietnamese restaurant of mine, Juniper Café. It's a light and flavorful salad loaded with crisp apples, juicy mango, and aromatic herbs, made even better with crunchy fried chicken nuggets, a perfect combination of the cuisines of Southeast Asia the American South. Freshness is the key here: Make sure you are using great produce and dress the salad as you fry those nuggets so that everything is at its peak.

2 cups (350 g) cooked Vietnamese rice vermicelli, chilled (4 ounces / 115 g dried)

1½ cups (70 g) shredded romaine lettuce

1 small carrot, cut into 2 by ¼-inch (5 cm by 6 mm) matchstick strips (about ¼ cup / 30 g)

½ small apple, peeled, cored, and cut into 2 by ¼-inch (5 cm by 6 mm) matchstick strips (about ¼ cup / 30 g)

½ medium cucumber, peeled, seeded, and cut into 2 by ¼-inch (5 cm by 6 mm) matchstick strips (about ¼ cup / 30 g)

½ mango, peeled, cored, and cut into 2 by ¼-inch (5 cm by 6 mm) matchstick strips (about ¼ cup / 30 g)

¼ small red onion, peeled, thinly sliced, and cut into 2 by ¼-inch (5 cm by 6 mm) matchstick strips (about ⅛ cup / 15 g)

15 mint leaves, torn

15 basil leaves, torn

20 cilantro leaves, torn

2 tablespoons Nuoc Cham (page 248)

2 tablespoons crushed peanuts, toasted

1 tablespoon fried shallots, homemade or store-bought (see Note)

1 tablespoon fried garlic, homemade or store-bought (see Note)

½ pound (225 g) Taiwanese Chicken Nuggets (page 193), hot from the fryer

In a large bowl, gently toss the vermicelli, lettuce, carrot, apple, cucumber, mango, onion, mint, basil, and cilantro. Add the nuoc cham and toss to combine.

Divide the salad between 2 bowls, top with the peanuts, fried shallots, fried garlic, and hot chicken nuggets, and serve immediately.

NOTE:

To make fried shallots or garlic, peel the shallot or garlic and use a mandoline to slice them about ⅛ inch (3 mm) thick. Set up a frying station. In a large, heavy pot set up with an oil thermometer, heat 2 inches (5 cm) vegetable oil over high heat to 300°F (150°C). Have a spider and paper towel–lined plate ready. Fry shallots or garlic until golden brown, 6 to 7 minutes for shallots and 4 to 5 minutes for garlic. Use the spider to transfer the shallots or garlic to the paper towel–lined plate, and sprinkle with salt to taste. When fully cooled, store in an airtight container in a warm, dry place. Save the oil for future use in salad dressings or marinades.

Pimiento Cheese and Pork Crispy Baos

MAKES 18 TO 22 BAOS, ENOUGH FOR 6 TO 8 AS AN APPETIZER

My mother often worked light, pillowy bao into our dumpling-making sessions at Hunan Village among the production of moo shu wrappers, scallion pancakes (see page 211), and the occasional chewy, sweet rice dumplings. This version updates the classic bao filling of ground pork, ginger, garlic, and other friends by inviting Southern pimiento cheese to the party, with the added twist of pan-frying them to get a deliciously crispy bottom (if you'd like a cheesier filling, simply increase the ratio of pimiento cheese to meat in the filling as desired). These are delicious served with Red Pepper Marmalade (page 243).

FOR THE DOUGH:

1 recipe milk bun dough from Steamed Milk Buns with Caviar-Buttermilk Sauce (page 231), prepared up to the point of rising

FOR THE FILLING:

12 ounces (340 g) lean ground pork

1 green onion, green and white parts, chopped

2 cloves garlic, minced

1 teaspoon minced fresh ginger

1 teaspoon toasted and ground fennel seed (see Note, page 227)

1 teaspoon toasted and ground cumin seed (see Note, page 227)

1 teaspoon toasted and ground star anise (see Note, page 227)

Salt and white pepper

½ cup (110 g) pimiento cheese from Pimiento Cheese with Scallion Pancakes (page 211), chilled

Canola oil

Make the dough and let rise until doubled as directed.

MEANWHILE, MAKE THE FILLING: In a large bowl, combine the pork, green onion, garlic, ginger, fennel, cumin, and star anise, season with salt and white pepper, and mix thoroughly. Cover and refrigerate until chilled, at least 30 minutes. When ready to proceed, place the bowl with the pork mixture in a larger bowl filled with ice. Add the chilled pimiento cheese to the pork mixture and mix with a rubber spatula until thoroughly combined, working quickly to keep everything as cold as possible. Cover and refrigerate until ready to proceed.

When the dough has risen, lightly dust a baking sheet with flour. Divide the dough into 12 to 16 even pieces (3 to 4 ounces / 85 to 115 g each) and roll into balls. Lay the balls on a work surface and flatten into a circle with the palm of your hand. Using a rolling pin, roll each piece of dough to roughly ¼-inch (6 mm) thickness with a 2-inch (5 cm) diameter.

Place roughly 2 tablespoons of the pork mixture in the center of each dough disk, then wrap the dough up and around the filling, pinching it together to create a series of pleats all around the edge of the disk until the bao is sealed.

Place the bao on the prepared baking sheet. Loosely cover the baking sheet with plastic wrap. Repeat with the remaining dough balls. Let the bao rest covered at room temperature for about 30 minutes before proceeding.

To cook the bao, heat 2 tablespoons canola oil in a large, lidded nonstick skillet over medium heat. Working in batches to avoid crowding, if necessary, place the bao in the pan, leaving roughly ½ inch (12 mm) of space in between each one.

When the pan is full, carefully pour enough water into the pan to submerge the bottom quarter of the bao and cover with the lid. When the dough has expanded and is fluffy and springy to the touch, the bao are done, 4 to 5 minutes. If an indention remains when the dough is lightly poked, add 2 tablespoons water, cover the pan, and cook for an additional 2 minutes. Repeat with any remaining bao and serve immediately.

Freeze any extra filled but uncooked bao in a single layer, then transfer them to a zip-top plastic bag and store them in the freezer for up to 3 months. Don't thaw before cooking—simply add a few minutes to the cooking time.

Crispy Pork Dumplings

MAKES 30 TO 36 DUMPLINGS, ENOUGH FOR 6 TO 8 AS AN APPETIZER

The ritual of sitting behind tubs of dough and mounds of meat making dumplings (aka potstickers) every Saturday at my mom's restaurant taught me the value of teamwork in a kitchen. Everyone pitched in to complete a task so seemingly arduous, but with a huge payoff in flavorful, filling dumplings in the end. As a kid, I first learned how to form the dumplings, focusing on the right amount of filling to put inside each wrapper, and how to properly fold and pleat each one. Once I mastered that, I was taught how to make the dough itself and shape it into wrappers. Finally, once I was well-practiced and old enough, I learned how to cook the dumplings in large batches using a three-tier metal steamer. The entire process taught me that each and every role in a restaurant is vital and has to be fulfilled properly in order for it all to come altogether.

Plus, the culture of the kitchen and camaraderie of the staff has always stayed with me. During the weekly six-hour dumpling sessions when we made about 1,200 dumplings, I learned the backstory of each employee as they told stories of where they came from, longing for the families they supported by sending money from afar. It taught me empathy, reinforcing my mother's inclusive approach to hospitality, reiterating to me that we are all one big family in the kitchen. Not to mention, this tough crew taught me all the necessary dirty kitchen words in Spanish, Mandarin, and Korean. And once they saw that I could produce the dumplings as fast as they could, I was no longer the boss lady's son, but a cook who could hang and hold his own.

Nowadays I make them with my wife and daughter—a decidedly less boisterous crew—to pass on the strong family tradition started so many years ago in my mother's kitchen. It's a cherished bit of family time where we all pitch in to do the work, sometimes doubling the batch and freezing extras to enjoy the fruits of our labors further down the road. We add a bit of water to the filling to make the dumplings juicier, just like my mom taught me way back when. And when we serve them, we often do so next to a soy-sesame sauce or Thai-style chili sauce, but in another nod to my childhood, a Southern-style pepper jelly has found its way onto our Atlanta table more than once.

recipe continues

FOR THE DOUGH:

2 cups (240 g) all-purpose flour, plus more for dusting

1 cup (240 ml) boiling water, plus more as needed

Pinch of salt

FOR THE FILLING:

1 pound (455 g) ground pork

½ cup (about 2 ounces / 45 g) finely chopped cabbage

2 cloves garlic, finely chopped

4 green onions, green and white parts finely chopped

1-inch (2.5 cm) piece fresh ginger, peeled and finely chopped

1 tablespoon toasted sesame oil

4½ teaspoons soy sauce

Salt and white pepper

2 tablespoons canola oil, plus more as needed

MAKE THE DOUGH: Place the flour in a large bowl, add ¼ cup (60 ml) boiling water, and stir with a wooden spoon to incorporate (see Note). The dough will look shaggy and dry. Stir another ¼ cup (60 ml) boiling water into the dough. It will be a bit less dry, but still shaggy. Add another ¼ cup (60 ml) boiling water to the dough and continue to mix with the wooden spoon. Once cool enough to handle, scrape any excess dough off the spoon and back into the bowl and knead the dough by hand until smooth. At this point, the dough should feel tacky, but not sticky. You shouldn't need more than ¾ cup (180 ml) boiling water, but if the dough still feels dry, add 1 tablespoon of boiling water at a time until the dough comes together as described. Shape the dough into a ball and place it in a bowl, cover with plastic wrap, and set aside at room temperature for 30 minutes.

MAKE THE FILLING: Place the pork, cabbage, garlic, green onions, ginger, sesame oil, soy sauce, salt and white pepper to taste, and 2 tablespoons water in a bowl and mix well to combine. Cover and refrigerate until ready to use.

Dust a baking sheet with flour and set aside. Shape the rested dough into a tube roughly ½ inch (12 mm) thick. Cut the tube crosswise into pieces roughly ½ inch (12 mm) wide. Using a rolling pin, roll each piece of dough into a disk roughly 3½ inches (9 cm) wide by ⅛ inch (3 mm) thick. Place a rough teaspoon of the filling in the middle of the dough disk. Fold the dough around the filling like a taco and pinch one end of the dough (whichever side is most comfortable for you) to begin to seal it. Holding the dumpling with your nondominant hand and keeping the bottom layer of dough flat, fold roughly ½ inch (12 mm) of the top layer of dough over onto itself toward the initial seal. Pinch this pleat to continue sealing the dumpling and repeat this process until the dumpling is completely sealed, making sure no air pockets remain inside the dumpling. Place the dumpling on the prepared baking sheet, and repeat this process with the remaining ingredients, making sure the dumplings are not touching each other on the baking sheet.

When ready to cook the dumplings, place the canola oil in a large, unheated nonstick skillet. Leaving at least ⅓ inch (8 mm) between each dumpling to allow for expansion while they cook, place as many dumplings as possible bottom down in the pan. Add water to the pan until the water reaches about halfway up the dumplings, then cover and place the pan over medium heat. Allow to cook until you start to hear a steady sizzle, 8 to 12 minutes, then remove the lid and carefully check the dumplings for golden brown bottoms, at which point they are ready. Transfer the dumplings to a serving platter and serve.

Freeze any extra filled but uncooked dumplings in a single layer, then transfer them to a zip-top plastic bag and store in the freezer for up to 3 months. Don't thaw before cooking—simply add a few minutes to the cooking time when using frozen dumplings

NOTE:

Using boiling water in this recipe softens the dough a bit more than cold or room temperature water, making it easier to stretch and fold when filling. Gradually adding the hot water allows the flour to hydrate more slowly and fully, and prevents using too much water, which would make the dough too sticky. Give yourself plenty of leeway when filling and sealing the dumplings. It isn't easy at first, but you will get the hang of it with practice.

Sriracha Spiced Baked Mac and Cheese with Panko Crust

SERVES 4 AS A MAIN COURSE OR 8 AS A SIDE

I've made a lot of mac and cheese in my day, from blue boxes of the instant variety to fancy lobster-filled versions. But my favorite will always be a Southern-style mac and cheese, upped with a bit of chile heat, thickened with egg, and baked to bubbling, golden brown perfection, complete with a crispy bread crumb–coated top. Growing up, we added spice with Louisiana's Tabasco or Crystal hot sauce, but even tastier is garlicky sriracha, which brings the fire without too much of the vinegar that a Southern hot sauce brings.

Butter, for greasing the pan

2 cups (8 ounces / 225 g) dry elbow macaroni, or any other short curly pasta

1 cup (240 ml) evaporated milk

½ cup (120 ml) whole milk

1 teaspoon onion powder

1 teaspoon garlic powder

2 cups (7 ounces / 200 g) shredded mild cheddar cheese, 1 tablespoon reserved

1 cup (3½ ounces / 100 g) shredded Colby-Jack cheese, 1 tablespoon reserved

1 cup (3½ ounces / 100 g) shredded Gruyère cheese, 1 tablespoon reserved

1 cup (3½ ounces / 100 g) shredded mozzarella cheese, 1 tablespoon reserved

4 sprigs thyme, leaves finely chopped

1 tablespoon sriracha, more or less as desired

½ cup (120 ml) sour cream

1 large egg, beaten

Salt and white pepper

2 tablespoons panko

Preheat the oven to 350°F (175°C) and grease a 9-inch (23 cm) square baking pan with butter. Set aside.

Fill a medium saucepan with water, place over high heat, and bring to a boil. Cook the macaroni as the label directs. Drain, rinse with cool water until cooled, transfer to a large bowl, and set aside.

In a medium saucepan, combine the evaporated milk, whole milk, onion powder, and garlic powder and bring to a simmer over medium-high heat. As soon as a simmer is reached, remove the pan from the heat and let cool slightly. Add to the pasta and stir to combine. Add all but the reserved 1 tablespoon of each of the cheeses, thyme, sriracha, sour cream, and egg, season with salt and white pepper, and fold until well combined, then transfer the mixture to the prepared baking pan.

Sprinkle with the panko and reserved cheeses, then bake until bubbly and golden brown, 30 to 45 minutes. Serve immediately. Refrigerate leftovers in an airtight container for up to 3 days.

Carbonara with Szechuan Peppercorns, Bacon, and Ramen Noodles

SERVES 2 AS A MAIN COURSE

Pasta carbonara was one of the first dishes I learned outside of our family restaurant when I went to culinary school in Australia, so it's fun to see how my version has adapted over the years with intriguingly numbing Szechuan peppercorns and the pungent depth of Chinese garlic chives while maintaining the basic technique of using the heat of the pasta to cook the raw egg into a silky-smooth sauce. Here, I've swapped out the traditional pancetta for bacon (I love smoky Benton's bacon produced just a few hours north in Tennessee) simply because it is always in my fridge, and instant ramen is an easy, rich noodle, but it can be swapped for a more traditional long pasta if you like.

4 slices thick-sliced bacon, cut into ¼-inch (6 mm) pieces

2 packages (3 ounces / 85 g each) dried instant ramen (reserve seasoning packets for another use)

1 large egg

1 large egg yolk

½ cup (2 ounces / 55 g) grated Parmesan cheese

1 tablespoon toasted and ground Szechuan peppercorns (see Note)

2 tablespoons finely chopped fresh Chinese garlic chives or standard fresh chives

Salt and black pepper

Fill a medium saucepan with water and bring to a boil over high heat.

Meanwhile, in a small skillet, cook the bacon over medium heat until golden brown and crispy, 4 to 6 minutes. Transfer the bacon to a large bowl (discard the rendered fat) and add the egg, egg yolk, cheese, Szechuan peppercorns, and garlic chives and mix well.

When the water is boiling, cook the ramen as the label directs. Reserve 2 tablespoons of the cooking water and drain the rest. Immediately add the hot ramen and reserved cooking water to the large bowl and quickly mix until the ingredients are incorporated. Season with salt and black pepper and serve immediately.

NOTE:

To toast the spices, heat in a 9-inch (23 cm) skillet over low heat until fragrant, 2 to 3 minutes. Let cool fully, then grind in a spice grinder or mortar and pestle.

Pad Thai with Roasted Georgia Peanuts

SERVES 2 AS A MAIN COURSE

This dish is an upgrade to the version experienced during my American upbringing at local Thai restaurants, moving more in the traditional direction by using tangy tamarind puree, umami-rich dried shrimp known as *kung haeng foi*, and the salted Thai radishes called *hua chai po*. The dried shrimp and salted radish are optional, but they make a big difference and can be found in Asian stores or online. As my Thai culinary schoolmate would say, "No Thai chef would make pad Thai without dried shrimp and salted radish!" Try to cook the noodles a bit less than usual, leaving them more al dente. During the stir-fry, they'll continue to cook as they soak up the liquid from the sauce and veggies.

FOR THE SAUCE:

1 tablespoon tamarind puree

1 tablespoon ketchup

1 teaspoon sugar

1 tablespoon oyster sauce

1 teaspoon fish sauce

FOR STIR-FRYING:

3 tablespoons canola oil

8 ounces (225 g) boneless skinless chicken breast, cut into ¼-inch (6 mm) thick slices

1 large egg, beaten

1 cup (90 g) plus ½ cup (45 g) bean sprouts

½ cup (80 g) sliced onion

¾ cup (3½ ounces / 100 g) Chinese garlic chives, cut into 1-inch (2.5 cm) pieces

3 cloves garlic, minced

1 tablespoon small dried shrimp, soaked in hot water for 10 minutes, then drained and chopped (optional)

1 tablespoon salted radish, soaked in hot water for 10 minutes, then drained and chopped (optional)

4 ounces (115 g) dried pad Thai rice noodles, cooked as the label directs, drained, and chilled

Salt and white pepper

2 tablespoons roasted Georgia peanuts, for serving

1 lime, cut into 4 wedges, for serving

recipe continues

MAKE THE SAUCE: In a small bowl, whisk the tamarind, ketchup, sugar, oyster sauce, and fish sauce and set aside.

MAKE THE STIR-FRY: In a wok or large skillet, heat 2 tablespoons of the oil over high heat. Add the chicken to the pan and cook, stirring constantly (stir-frying), until lightly browned and cooked through, about 2 minutes. Remove the chicken from the pan and set aside.

Add the remaining 1 tablespoon oil to the pan, and once it starts to smoke, add the egg and stir-fry until scrambled, 10 to 20 seconds.

Add ½ cup (45 g) bean sprouts, the onion, garlic chives, and garlic and stir-fry until slightly fragrant with a little color, 1½ to 2 minutes.

Add the cooked chicken and dried shrimp and salted radish, if using, to the pan and stir-fry for another 30 seconds. Add the noodles and sauce and stir-fry for 1 more minute, then adjust the seasoning with salt and white pepper (if you'd like the noodles to soften a bit, add 1 tablespoon water and cook for another 30 seconds to 1 minute; repeat as necessary to achieve desired noodle texture).

Divide the noodles between 2 bowls and garnish with the remaining 1 cup (90 g) bean sprouts, the peanuts, and a couple lime wedges. Serve immediately.

Steamed Milk Buns with Caviar-Buttermilk Sauce

SERVES 2 TO 4 AS AN APPETIZER

I've been making versions of this bun for more than three decades now, using the dough as a stand-alone item in place of bread, rolled thin as a wrapper for pan-steamed dumplings, or as a steamed bun stuffed with pork. My riffing all started in the dumpling-making sessions at Hunan Village, where from time to time my mother would make us special off-menu bao variations stuffed with things like ground pork, veggies, or boiled eggs. Other times, she would pan-steam the bao, which, unlike a simply steamed dumpling, gives them a crunchy bottom like the Crispy Pork Dumplings on page 221. This would inspire me later in my career, from early days at the tapas bar I worked at during college in Athens where we made steamed buns filled with ground pork, to my failed attempts at getting bao filled with a bouillabaisse-flavored gelatin that would turn into a soup dumpling once cooked on the menu at Le Bernardin. Nowadays, I often prefer to fill bao with a combination of ground pork and pimiento cheese (page 218), or simply to pair the soft, warm buns with caviar, like we do at Lazy Betty and in the recipe below. They make a nice upgrade from the standard blini, as do the scallion pancakes on page 211. If you tend to like a lot of sauce, simply double its recipe.

FOR THE MILK BUNS:

⅔ cup (165 ml) whole milk

½ teaspoon instant dry yeast

1½ cups (180 g) all-purpose flour

¼ teaspoon baking powder

1½ teaspoons sugar

1¼ tablespoons unsalted butter, at room temperature

Cooking oil spray

FOR THE CAVIAR-BUTTERMILK SAUCE:

½ cup (120 ml) full-fat buttermilk

2 tablespoons cream cheese

Zest of ½ lemon (about 1½ teaspoons)

Salt

3 tablespoons thinly sliced chives, ½ teaspoon reserved for garnish

1 ounce (28 g) caviar, trout roe, or salmon roe (smoked if desired)

MAKE THE MILK BUNS: Place the milk in a small bowl and heat in the microwave in 10-second intervals until just warm to the touch. Stir in the yeast and allow it to proof until the yeast gives off bubbles that float to the top of the milk.

Meanwhile, place the flour, baking powder, and sugar in a large bowl and whisk together.

When the yeast is proofed, add the milk mixture to the dry ingredients and mix together with a spoon or chopsticks, adding in the butter when the dough is still crumbly. Transfer the dough to a work surface and knead with your hands until a smooth ball forms, 6 to 8 minutes. Place the dough in a bowl, cover with a damp towel in a slightly warm place (the microwave works great), and allow the dough to rise until doubled in size, 1 to 2 hours.

When ready to proceed, cut 8 pieces of parchment paper, each roughly 3 inches (7.5 cm) square. Spray each square with oil spray. Divide the dough into 8 equal pieces (1 ounce / 28 g each) and roll into balls, then place each ball on a prepared parchment square. Spray each ball with oil spray, then loosely cover the batch of balls with a piece of plastic wrap. Allow the dough to double in size, 1 to 2 hours.

Prepare a bamboo steamer setup and, working in batches if necessary, place the dough balls and the parchment they are on onto the steamer, leaving enough room for the buns to rise. Steam, covered, until the buns are cooked through, 8 to 10 minutes, adding water to the steamer as needed. Repeat as needed and set the cooked buns aside.

MAKE THE CAVIAR-BUTTERMILK SAUCE: Place the buttermilk, cream cheese, lemon zest, and salt to taste in a medium bowl and whisk until combined, 10 to 15 seconds. Add the chives and caviar and gently fold in until incorporated. Adjust the seasoning as needed, transfer to a serving dish, and garnish with the reserved ½ teaspoon chives.

Reheat the buns in the steamer for a few minutes, then serve the warm buns immediately with the sauce, tearing the soft buns and dipping into the sauce to get chunks of caviar and chives.

Japchae with Sorghum-Ginger Sauce

SERVES 2 AS A MAIN COURSE

Japchae is a classic cold Korean dish comprised of noodles made from sweet potato starch (not to be confused with the mung bean noodles often used in China), loaded with vegetables. The noodles are chewy, yet soft, and maintain their pleasing texture in both hot and cold preparations. This modern version replaces sugar with sorghum for a richer, more complex flavor, and I've also swapped the usual spinach for the hearty Southern green collards, which will allow the dish to stand up for a few days in the refrigerator. To beef the recipe up, add a few thinly sliced Grilled Mandarin Beef Ribs (page 159) to each bowl, and serve with your favorite chili crunch if desired.

1 tablespoon canola oil, plus more as needed

½ cup (56 g) thinly sliced collard greens, stems removed

Salt and white pepper

1 large carrot, peeled and cut into 1 by ⅛-inch (2.5 cm by 3 mm) matchstick strips (½ cup / 60 g)

½ cup (75 g) thinly sliced white onion

1 zucchini, cut into ½-inch (12 mm) strips

1 red bell pepper, cut into ½-inch (12 mm) strips

2 green onions, green and white parts cut into 1-inch (2.5 cm) pieces

2 tablespoons sorghum syrup

1 tablespoon soy sauce

1 clove garlic, finely minced

1½ teaspoons finely minced fresh ginger

1½ teaspoons toasted sesame oil

1 tablespoon toasted sesame seeds

4 ounces (115 g) dried sweet potato/japchae noodles, cooked as the label directs, drained, and chilled

¼ cup (22 g) reconstituted and thinly sliced wood ear mushrooms (3 g dried)

In a medium skillet, heat the canola oil over medium-high heat. Add the collard greens, season with salt and white pepper, and cook, stirring occasionally, just until they begin to soften, 2 to 3 minutes. Remove the collard greens from the pan, then repeat this process, cooking the carrot, onion, zucchini, red bell pepper, and green onions one ingredient at a time, adding oil as needed if the pan becomes too dry. When complete, refrigerate the vegetables in an airtight container until they are cold or for up to 24 hours, until you are ready to assemble the dish.

In a large bowl, whisk the sorghum syrup, soy sauce, garlic, ginger, sesame oil, and sesame seeds until combined. Add the cooked noodles to the bowl, toss to coat them in the sauce, and let sit for about 10 minutes to soak up the sauce, tossing a couple times.

Add the chilled vegetables and mushrooms and gently toss to combine. Split between 2 bowls and serve immediately, refrigerating any extra for up to 1 week.

Stir-Fried Egg Noodles with Collard Greens and Eggs

SERVES 2 AS A MAIN COURSE

This recipe takes the stir-fried noodles of my youth and fortifies them with collard greens and carrots, but you could easily add bok choy, cabbage, chicken, or shrimp as well. Top with a hot sauce of your liking such as sambal oelek.

2 tablespoons oyster sauce

1½ teaspoons soy sauce

1½ teaspoons toasted sesame oil

1 tablespoon Shaoxing cooking wine

4 tablespoons canola oil

4 large eggs, beaten

2 cloves garlic, minced

1 tablespoon minced fresh ginger

½ cup (60 g) onions cut into 2 by ¼-inch (5 cm by 6 mm) matchstick strips

½ cup (60 g) carrots cut into 2 by ¼-inch (5 cm by 6 mm) matchstick strips

10 ounces (280 g) Chinese egg noodles, cooked as the label directs, cooled in water, drained, tossed with 1 teaspoon canola oil, and chilled

8 ounces (225 g) collard greens, cleaned and chopped (2 cups loosely packed)

Salt and white pepper

In a small bowl, combine the oyster sauce, soy sauce, sesame oil, and Shaoxing cooking wine. Set aside.

In a wok or skillet, heat 2 tablespoons of the canola oil over medium-high heat. When thin wisps of smoke rise from the pan, add the eggs and cook until scrambled, 1 to 2 minutes. Transfer the eggs to a plate and set aside.

Wipe the pan clean with a paper towel, return to medium heat, and add the remaining 2 tablespoons canola oil. Once the oil starts to shimmer, add the garlic, ginger, onions, and carrots and cook, stirring frequently (stir-frying), until slightly soft, 2 to 3 minutes.

Add the cooked noodles to the pan and stir-fry with the vegetables until heated through, about 2 minutes. Add the collard greens, oyster sauce mixture, and reserved scrambled eggs and stir-fry for another 2 minutes. Adjust the seasoning with salt and white pepper and serve immediately.

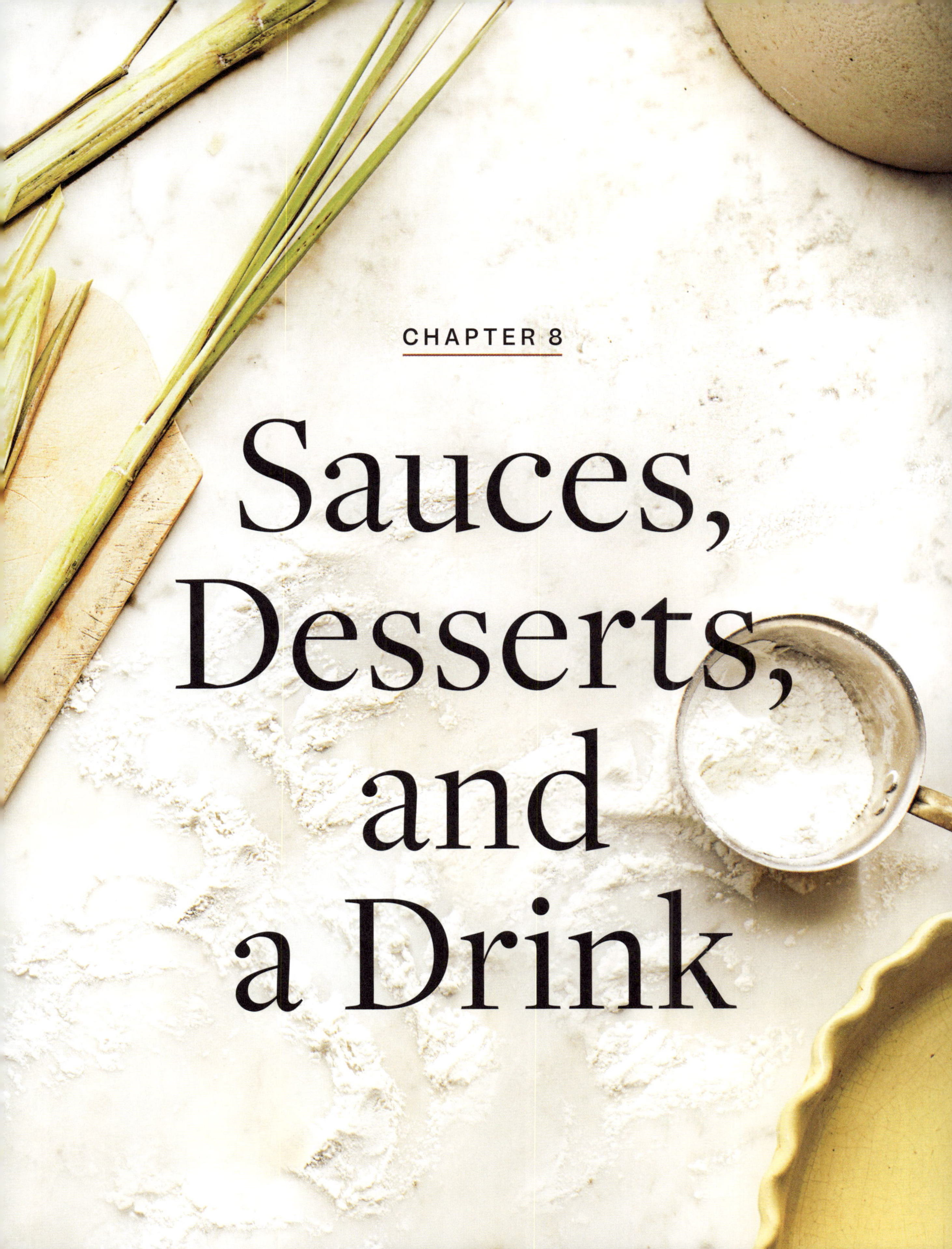

CHAPTER 8

Sauces, Desserts, and a Drink

Travel

Although I am from the American South, many of my culinary influences have come through my travels. My mantra at Lazy Betty is to "find harmony on a plate," so we're always pushing the boundaries of the food we serve, and it's possible that a single dish will have input from four or five different countries as we embrace the challenge of bringing seemingly dissimilar flavors and techniques together into a cohesive, balanced, and delicious recipe.

My travels throughout Asia have been the most influential on my cooking. I've been through Thailand, Vietnam, Malaysia, and Singapore, but none of those trips have impacted me as much as the time I've spent in China and Japan.

From the Peking duck and steamed buns of the northern Chinese cities of Beijing and Tianjin to the majestically beautiful southern city of Guilin with its karst-filled landscape and fresh-killed chicken cooked in wine and ginger, to the wok hei–rich dishes of hot Hong Kong street stalls, travel has built on the heritage inherited from my Chinese parents.

In Japan, I've eaten spectacular food and learned how to dispatch and butcher a live turtle and fillet an eel with a spike and eel knife at my good friend Shinichiro Takagi's two-Michelin-star kaiseki restaurant, Zeniya, in Kanazawa. But Japan was about more than just food for me. It was how every single detail of a dining experience is completely intentional, from the lively izakayas rich with the aroma of grilling meats to the blindingly fast takoyaki cooks to Michelin three-star dinners at Kikunoi and Tempura Matsu.

The flavors, techniques, and ethics from these far-away lands come back with me every time I return home, but more importantly, the connection to others and different ways of life sticks with me as I aim to transcend cultural boundaries by bringing people together over food. And it's not just at Lazy Betty that I hope to see this happen. I'm hoping this book brings some cultural insight to your home kitchen, and that you're able to incorporate some of the influences I've been exposed to during my travels, as well as during my life here in the South. After all, it's the differences that lie within us that can make life beautiful—and food delicious.

OPPOSITE, CLOCKWISE FROM TOP LEFT: A ham stand in the Boqueria Market in Barcelona; a "rice paper" pizza from a food cart in Da Nang; a variety of dried seafood from a shop in Hong Kong; a spread of fresh produce in Taiwan.

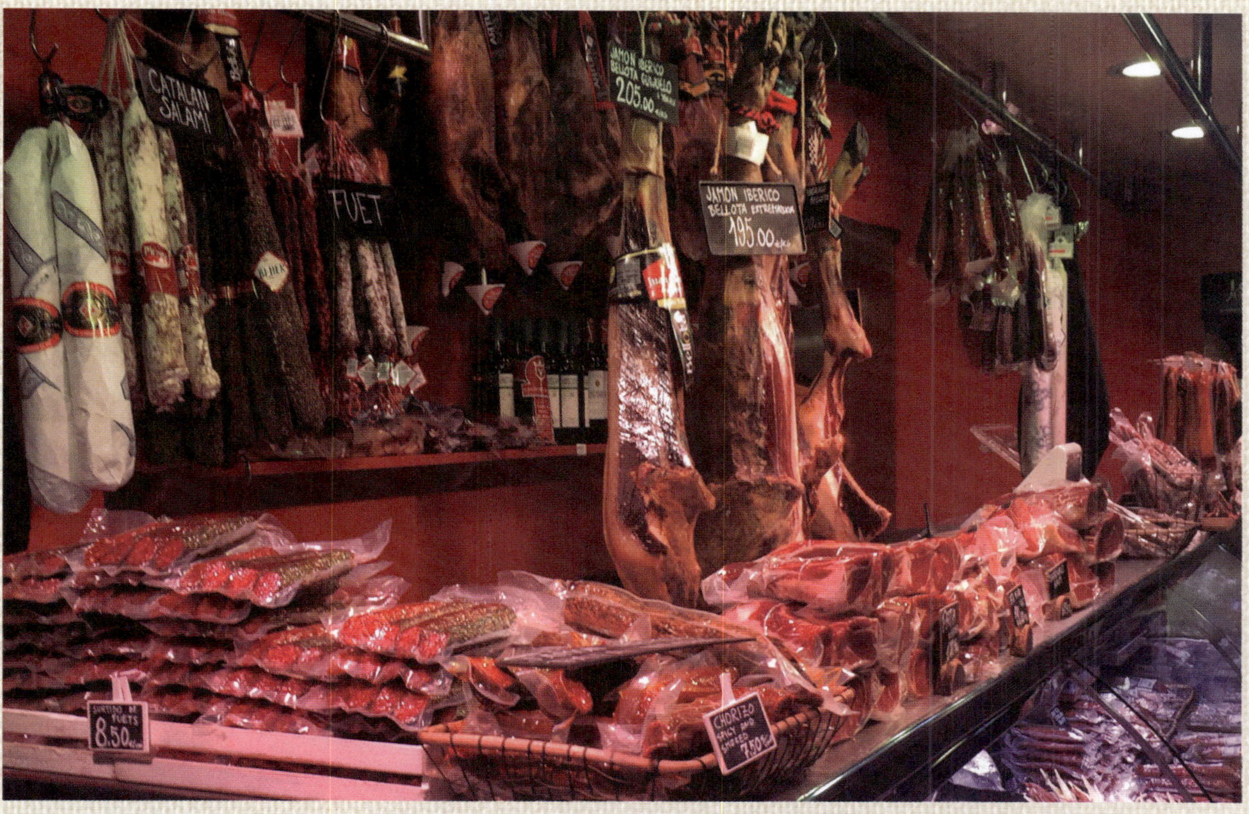
CATALAN SALAMI
FUET
JAMON IBERICO
195.00
8.50

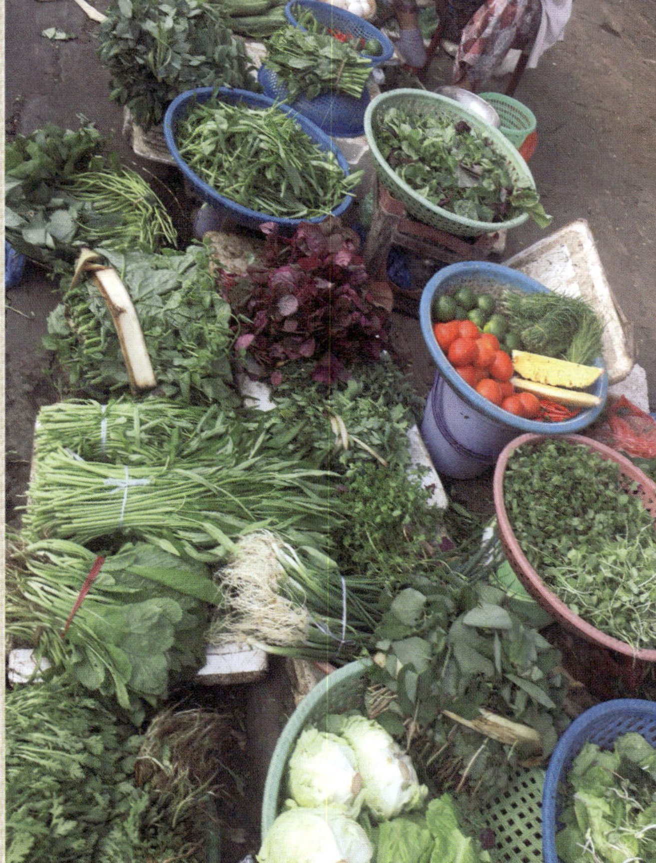

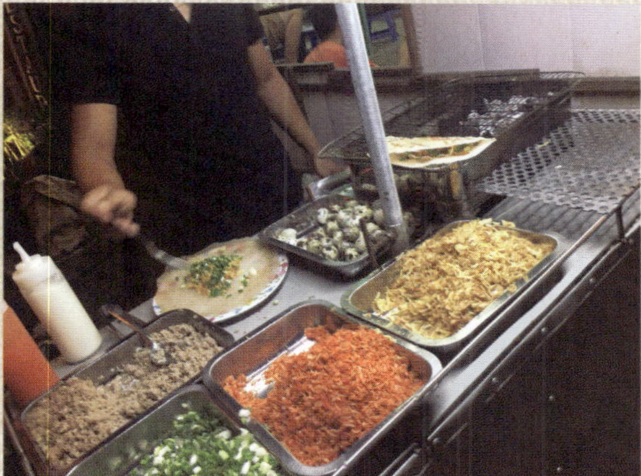

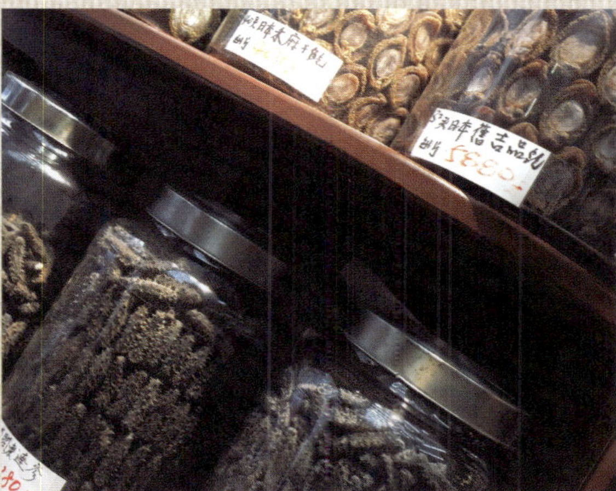

Red Pepper Marmalade

MAKES ABOUT 2 CUPS (480 ML)

Some type of sweet chili sauce has always been present in my life, and they've all contributed to this recipe. First, I grew up eating Mae Ploy Thai Sweet Chili Sauce as a dip for things like crispy crab Rangoon at Hunan Village. Later, in culinary school in Australia, I learned how to make a homemade version of the sauce from my Thai classmates, a rendition I'd later serve with pork-filled wontons during my time as the executive chef at Le Colonial in New York.

Then, I was introduced to a citrusy marmalade that reminded me of sweet chili sauce when, on a culinary trip for Eric Ripert Consulting, I visited Westend Bistro in Washington, DC, where it was served as a condiment for a pimiento cheese spread. Finally, when opening my restaurant Juniper Café (a *Bon Appétit* best new restaurant in 2023 that has since closed), we were contemplating buying vs. making sweet chili sauce when our lead baker Robin offered her recipe. When it turned out to be a red pepper marmalade similar to the one that I tasted in DC, stars aligned. This recipe is my version that draws on all of those inspirations, with the familiar sweet flavor and bright red color of a store-bought red chili sauce and the bright tangy freshness of a marmalade. Use it to dip Taiwanese Chicken Nuggets (page 193), alongside Fried Catfish with Sauce Chirizu (page 146) in lieu of the sauce chirizu, or with Pimiento Cheese Wontons (page 208), Crispy Pork Dumplings (page 221), Pimiento Cheese and Pork Crispy Baos (page 218), or the Cornmeal-Crusted Fried Chinese Eggplant (page 28), and much more.

8 red bell peppers, seeded and roughly chopped (2½ to 3 cups / 1120 g)

½ cup (120 ml) sorghum syrup

½ cup (100 g) sugar

⅓ cup (75 ml) distilled white vinegar

1 tablespoon minced fresh ginger

1 tablespoon minced garlic

1 teaspoon salt

Zest and juice of 1 lime (about 1 teaspoon zest and 2 tablespoons juice)

In a food processor, pulse the red peppers to a chunky pulp, about 5 pulses.

Transfer the peppers to a medium saucepan and add the sorghum syrup, sugar, vinegar, ginger, garlic, salt, and 1 cup (240 ml) water. Place over medium-low heat and bring to a simmer. Continue to cook, stirring frequently with a rubber spatula, until reduced by roughly one-third, 12 to 15 minutes.

Remove from the heat and stir in the lime zest and juice. Cool completely, then transfer to an airtight container and store in the refrigerator for up to 3 weeks.

Char Siu Marinade

MAKES ABOUT 2 CUPS (480 ML)

Char siu (which originated in the Canton region of China) is now the most ubiquitous form of barbecue pork in Asia, found in Thailand, Vietnam, Malaysia, all over China, and in Chinese restaurants around the world. I've seen it served from a food cart; I've eaten it in Michelin-starred restaurants. My version is fairly traditional, but includes sorghum syrup, which not only adds a deep complex flavor beyond that of sugar, but also bulks up the yield of the marinade. Many modern recipes add red food coloring in place of the red fermented tofu, but a traditional char siu shouldn't be a pure red. It's more of a reddish-amber from the red fermented tofu. This recipe will make enough for three batches of Char Siu Glazed Baby Back Ribs (page 110), and you can also brush it on chicken, pork chops, or wherever you might like a sweet, delicious bolt of flavor.

2 cubes red fermented tofu plus 1½ teaspoons juice, about ½ ounce (14 g) tofu and juice total (see Note)

2 tablespoons Chinese five-spice powder

½ teaspoon garlic powder

½ teaspoon onion powder

½ teaspoon ginger powder

½ cup (120 ml) soy sauce

¼ cup (60 ml) sorghum syrup

6 tablespoons (90 ml) hoisin sauce

2 teaspoons toasted sesame oil

2 tablespoons bourbon

In a medium bowl, break up the tofu with a fork until very crumbly. Add the Chinese five-spice powder, garlic powder, onion powder, ginger powder, soy sauce, sorghum syrup, hoisin sauce, sesame oil, and bourbon and whisk until combined. Use as directed in the recipe (such as Char Siu Glazed Baby Back Ribs on page 110 or Char Siu Pulled Pork on page 113), and refrigerate any leftover marinade, tightly sealed, for up to 3 months.

NOTE:

Red fermented tofu is essentially a cheat code when incorporated into a dish, providing great umami depth and a tasty bit of funkiness. It can be utilized as a condiment on dishes like Bacon Congee and Poached Eggs (page 82), or as a quick flavor bomb when crumbled in or on dishes. It may be too pungent to eat by itself, but it can complement other ingredients. As a fermented product, it can last indefinitely when properly stored, and it's easy to find in Asian markets or online.

Char siu
4/1
WECK

mala oil 4/2

Mala Oil

MAKES 1½ CUPS (360 ML)

Mala is a Chinese term meaning numbing (*ma*) and hot (*la*), referring to the effects of Szechuan peppercorns and Szechuan chili, respectively. This pantry staple is full of that beguiling sensation and is what we call a "workhorse" in a professional kitchen: simple to make, easily scaled to large quantities, with many uses. It can be used in a vinaigrette for the Cucumber and Tomato Salad with Mala-Buttermilk Dressing (page 40), as a dipping sauce for the Crispy Pork Dumplings (page 221), as a finishing oil on the Lemon Pepper Ramen with Shredded Chicken (page 213), or drizzled over anything to boost its flavor and heat. I always have a jar of Mala Oil in my fridge at home.

3 tablespoons Szechuan chili flakes (see Note, page 29)

4½ teaspoons Szechuan peppercorns

4 star anise pods

2 black cardamom pods

1 cinnamon stick

1 tablespoon fennel seeds

1 teaspoon whole cloves

4½ teaspoons sesame seeds

2 cloves garlic, finely minced

1 tablespoon minced ginger

1 cup (240 ml) canola oil

½ cup (100 g) rendered beef tallow (see Note)

1 tablespoon toasted sesame oil

In a medium skillet, toast the Szechuan chili flakes, Szechuan peppercorns, star anise, black cardamom, cinnamon stick, fennel seeds, and cloves over medium heat, stirring constantly until fragrant, 45 to 60 seconds. Remove the spices from the pan and let cool, then grind in a spice grinder or blender until coarsely ground. Transfer the spices to a medium heatproof bowl and add the sesame seeds, garlic, and ginger. Set aside.

In a small saucepan, heat the canola oil and tallow over medium heat until thin whisps of smoke appear, 1 to 2 minutes, then pour over the spices and stir to combine.

Let cool to room temperature, then add the sesame oil and transfer to a jar for storage. Refrigerate in an airtight container for up to 6 months.

NOTE:

Tallow is simply rendered beef fat, and it really takes this oil to the next level. Good butchers often sell it, or you can make it yourself. If you have access to smoked tallow, all the better; ask your favorite barbecue spot if they've got any available. If you don't have beef tallow lying around, just substitute an equal amount of additional canola oil in its place.

Nuoc Cham

MAKES 1 CUP (240 ML)

Nuoc cham is a sauce frequently used in Vietnamese cooking, and though recipes and versions change from town to town and cook to cook, I favor this one for its versatility. Use it in the Braised Romaine with Nuoc Cham Caesar (page 35), Mandarin Beef and Papaya Salad with Roasted Peanuts (page 160), or Shrimp Toast (page 139), or to simply dress greens or shredded green papaya. Its shelf life is indefinite, and it gets even better the longer it is stored.

½ cup (120 ml) fish sauce

1 clove garlic, minced

1 tablespoon minced ginger

1 teaspoon sambal oelek

Zest and juice of 1 lime (about 1 teaspoon zest and 2 tablespoons juice)

2 tablespoons sorghum syrup

Combine the fish sauce, garlic, ginger, sambal, lime zest and juice, sorghum syrup, and ¼ cup (60 ml) water in a small bowl and whisk to combine. Transfer to a jar and refrigerate indefinitely.

15 ml
5 ml

“Ronald” Palmer

MAKES 1 GALLON (3.8 L), ENOUGH FOR ABOUT 12 SERVINGS

This is my spin on a traditional Arnold Palmer, adding an unexpected depth with lemongrass and floral notes with pandan and chrysanthemum tea. My mother used to make chrysanthemum tea on the regular; it's not as tannic as traditional black Southern tea, and it contains no caffeine. It's the tea they serve you hot at dim sum, but I always drank it cold at home, refreshing during hot Georgia summers. If you'd like, feel free to spike it with a splash of vodka, white rum, or tequila.

2 stalks lemongrass

4 ounces (115 g) chrysanthemum tea leaves

2 (6-inch / 15 cm) pandan leaves (see Note, page 256)

½ cup (100 g) sugar, plus more if desired

1 gallon (3.8 L) boiling water

Juice of 6 lemons (about 9 ounces / 270 ml), plus more if desired

Cut each lemongrass stalk in half crosswise and discard the top half. Remove the tough outer leaves of the remaining 2 halves, then cut each half in half lengthwise. Using the back of a chef's knife, hit each piece of lemongrass several times to bruise it and release its aroma and oils.

Place the bruised lemongrass in a glass pitcher, then add the tea leaves, pandan leaves, sugar, and boiling water and stir until the sugar has dissolved. Allow to steep until the tea cools to room temperature, 30 to 45 minutes, then stir in the lemon juice.

Taste and add more sugar and/or lemon juice if desired, then serve over ice. Refrigerate any extra tightly sealed for up to 1 week.

Fried Bananas with Ice Cream

SERVES 2 TO 4 AS A DESSERT

This quick classic from my mom's restaurant was one of my favorite desserts growing up. The bananas get soft and creamy, the wrappers add a crisp, toasted quality, and best of all, it's fun and easy to make with my daughter.

2 ripe medium bananas

2 tablespoons brown sugar

1 tablespoon Chinese five-spice powder

8 spring roll wrappers

1 large egg, beaten

¼ cup (60 ml) canola oil

Vanilla ice cream, for serving

Honey, for serving

Peel the bananas, then cut them in half lengthwise. Cut each piece in half crosswise and place them in a medium bowl. Add the sugar and Chinese five-spice powder and toss to combine. Place 1 spring roll wrapper on a cutting board so it looks like a diamond (rather than a square). Place 1 piece of banana in the center of the diamond so that each end of the banana faces toward the right and left points of the wrapper. Brush a bit of egg on the bottom point of the diamond, then fold the right and left points in and over the banana. Brush a bit of egg on the top point of the diamond, then starting from the bottom point, roll the wrapper up all the way to the top, making sure the package is completely sealed. Repeat with the remaining bananas and wrappers.

In a 10-inch (25 cm) skillet, heat the oil over medium heat. When the oil is hot and begins to shimmer, place the banana rolls in the pan. Working in batches as necessary to avoid overcrowding, cook until the rolls are golden brown on one side, about 1 minute. Flip the banana rolls and brown the other side for another minute, then transfer to a paper towel–lined plate. Repeat this process until all pieces are browned, adding more oil to the pan as needed. Divide the banana rolls among the desired number of serving bowls and top with a scoop of vanilla ice cream and a drizzle of honey. Serve immediately.

Pandan Banana Pudding

SERVES 4 TO 6 AS A DESSERT

As a kid, I'd frequently spread kaya, a rich, pale green spread made with coconut milk, eggs, and pandan leaf (see Note) on toast or steamed buns as a snack. Just as often, I'd dive into one of the South's most iconic desserts, banana pudding. As an adult, I thought "why not mix the two?"

You'll be producing a mega-cream from two types of creams for this dessert—these are creams you have likely eaten before and maybe have made yourself, even if you don't recognize the names commonly used in professional kitchens. First, make a simple custard known as *pastry cream*, then make Chantilly cream (a fancy name for sweetened, whipped cream). Combine the two, and you've got a rich, stable diplomat cream.

These creams may sound like a lot of work, but the flavor is richer and purer than store-bought pudding mixes, and once you make them, they'll prove valuable for other cream-filled desserts, like trifles, eclairs, even doughnuts.

FOR THE PASTRY CREAM:

2 large eggs

2 large egg yolks

⅓ cup (40 g) cornstarch

¾ cup (150 g) sugar

Pinch of salt

1 teaspoon vanilla extract

2 cups (480 ml) whole milk

2 tablespoons unsalted butter, cut into 6 small pieces and chilled

FOR THE CHANTILLY CREAM:

1¼ cups (300 ml) heavy cream, chilled

1 tablespoon sugar

1½ teaspoons pandan extract

1 (11-ounce / 310 g) box vanilla wafers

3 ripe bananas, thinly sliced

MAKE THE PASTRY CREAM: In a medium bowl, whisk the eggs, yolks, cornstarch, sugar, salt, and vanilla until combined, then set aside.

Place the milk in a small saucepan over medium-high heat and bring to a simmer. While whisking, pour about one-third of the hot milk into the egg mixture. Once fully incorporated, whisk another one-third of the hot milk into the egg mixture. Repeat with the final one-third of the hot milk and return the pot to the stove over medium-low heat.

Bring to a simmer, stirring slowly but constantly with a rubber spatula to prevent bubbles and making sure to stir the bottom and corners of the saucepan to prevent burning, 3 to 4 minutes. The pastry cream will thicken during this time. Remove from the heat and stir in the cold butter until it is melted and incorporated. Cover the custard with plastic wrap directly on its surface and refrigerate for at least 4 hours or up to overnight.

MEANWHILE, MAKE THE CHANTILLY CREAM: Place the heavy cream and sugar in a large bowl and whisk until soft peaks form (you can also use a stand mixer). Add the pandan extract to the Chantilly cream and gently fold to incorporate. Cover with plastic wrap and chill if not immediately proceeding.

recipe continues

When the pastry cream is chilled, fold it until smooth again. Gently fold in the pandan-infused Chantilly cream thoroughly, then transfer to a piping bag or zip-top plastic bag and set aside.

Place about 6 vanilla wafers in a zip-top plastic bag and crush with a rolling pin (shoot for about ¼ cup / 30 g finely crushed wafer crumbs) and set aside.

In a 9-inch (23 cm) square casserole dish, lay a single layer of whole vanilla wafers followed by a single layer of sliced bananas. Pipe the combined cream on top of the wafers (if using a zip-top plastic bag, simply cut about ½ inch / 12 mm of one corner of the bag off for a makeshift piping bag) until the wafers are completely covered, then smooth the cream out with a rubber spatula. Add another layer of vanilla wafers and bananas, then repeat the cream process. Garnish with the reserved crushed wafers and serve immediately, or refrigerate for up to 1 week.

NOTE:

Distinctly herbaceous and delicate, pandan is often found in Asian desserts but also finds itself in savory dishes like Hainanese Chicken Rice Rice (page 68). Typically, it's used to infuse a dish and is removed before eating; extracts are also widely available in Asian markets and online.

Blueberry and Lemongrass Pie

SERVES ABOUT 8 AS A DESSERT

This pie was developed in response to my wife and daughter's love of a perfect blueberry pie—the filling simultaneously sweet and tart, the crust flaky yet tender—and a summer spent eating boatloads of them while traveling through Maine at peak blueberry season. Back home, we head twenty minutes southeast of my hometown of Stockbridge, Georgia, to Southern Belle Farm to pick their irresistible late May and June blueberries for a blueberry pie for my wife's birthday. Heavily influenced by my time as the executive chef of the Vietnamese restaurant Le Colonial in New York, I opened a spot in Atlanta called Juniper Café, where we embraced the use of unexpected ingredients like floral lemongrass and assertive Vietnamese cinnamon (aka Saigon cinnamon) in our blueberry pies, loving the at once familiar and exotic notes they brought to the pie. The café is now closed, but this creative representation of those ideal Maine blueberry pies was wildly popular during its time.

Later, after introducing a pithivier (a savory pie) to the menu at Lazy Betty, I found that brushing egg wash on a crust, then allowing it to dry out in the fridge or freezer for a few hours really helps create a wonderful sheen and even browning. One more tip: A glass pie dish lets you monitor the bottom of the pie just as easily as the top. If the top is browning too fast for your liking, simply cover the pie loosely with aluminum foil for the remainder of the bake.

FOR THE CRUST:

2½ cups (300 g) all-purpose flour, plus more for dusting

1 teaspoon salt

1 teaspoon sugar

8 ounces (225 g) unsalted butter, cut into ½-inch (12 mm) cubes and chilled

8 tablespoons (120 ml) ice water

FOR THE FILLING:

2 pounds (32 ounces / 910 g) fresh blueberries

¼ cup (28 g) cornstarch

½ cup (100 g) plus 2 tablespoons sugar

Pinch of salt

1½ teaspoons ground Vietnamese cinnamon

Zest and juice of 1 lemon (about 1 tablespoon zest and 3 tablespoons juice)

1 stalk lemongrass, top one-third removed, outer layer removed, and finely minced

2 tablespoons unsalted butter

2 tablespoons heavy cream

1 large egg yolk

1½ teaspoons turbinado sugar

recipe continues

MAKE THE CRUST: In a food processor, place the flour, salt, sugar, and cold butter and pulse until it resembles moist and clumpy sand. Add the ice water one tablespoon at a time, pulsing after each addition, just until the dough comes together (take care not to overwork the dough). Remove the dough and separate it into 2 portions, one roughly 60 percent and one 40 percent of the dough mass.

Place each portion on a lightly floured work surface and roll into 2 disks, each roughly ½ inch (12 mm) thick. Wrap each disk in plastic wrap and refrigerate for at least 1 hour, or freeze for up to 1 month until ready to use (if you freeze the dough, allow it to sit at room temperature for about 1 hour before assembling the pie).

MAKE THE FILLING: In a large saucepan, combine about 1 cup (5 ounces / 150 g) of the blueberries, the cornstarch, sugar, salt, cinnamon, lemon zest and juice, lemongrass, butter, and 1 tablespoon water over medium heat. Bring to a simmer, stirring frequently until the filling thickens, about 4 minutes. Remove from the heat and pour into a large bowl, then add the remaining 5 cups (27 ounces / 760 g) blueberries and stir to combine. Cover with plastic wrap and refrigerate until completely cool and set, at least 1 hour.

When ready to proceed, make an egg wash by beating the heavy cream and egg yolk in a small bowl.

Remove the dough disks from the refrigerator. Place the disks on a lightly floured surface and roll the larger one to a rough 11-inch (28 cm) diameter and the smaller one to a 10-inch (25 cm) diameter. Lay the larger disk into a 9-inch (23 cm) glass pie dish, making sure the dough is snugly inside the pie dish.

Pour the chilled filling into the dish. Brush a bit of the egg wash on any overhanging dough, then place the smaller dough on top of the pie, pressing any overlapping dough together. Use a fork to crimp the overlapping dough together around the entire rim of the pie, cutting off any excess dough. Brush the entire top of the pie with the egg wash.

Cut four S-shaped slits roughly 1½ inches (4 cm) each from the center of the pie toward the edge to serve as steam vents, then sprinkle the turbinado sugar on the pie. Refrigerate the pie until it is fully chilled again, at least 1 hour or up to overnight.

When ready to proceed, preheat the oven to 400°F (205°C).

Place the chilled pie on a baking sheet and bake the pie until golden brown on top and bottom, 45 to 60 minutes, rotating the pie once halfway through cooking. Remove the pie from the oven and allow to cool completely, about 2 hours. Slice and serve, refrigerating any leftover pie for up to 1 week.

Vietnamese Coffee Tiramisu

SERVES 6 TO 8 AS A DESSERT

During my time as chef at Le Colonial in New York, I'd drink a Vietnamese coffee once a day and loved it. The robust flavor of the deeply roasted arabica and robusta beans centered me in the same way it centers this tiramisu, with bitter notes balancing out the sweet richness of mascarpone cheese and sweetened condensed milk as in a Vietnamese iced coffee. If you want to adjust the intensity of the coffee flavor either way, simply adjust the strength of the coffee you use—I like the heavy concentration of a double dose. Finally, keep the eggs and dairy products cold for best results while whipping them.

FOR THE COFFEE:

3 servings (1 cup / 240 ml) instant Vietnamese coffee, double strength, hot (preferably 2 packets of Trung Nguyen brand's G7 made with 1 cup / 240 ml hot water)

2 tablespoons unsweetened Dutch-process cocoa

2 teaspoons ground Vietnamese cinnamon

1 tablespoon vanilla extract

FOR THE CREAM:

5 large egg yolks

⅓ cup (70 g) sugar

1 pound (455 g) mascarpone cheese, chilled

1¾ cups (420 ml) heavy cream

Salt

25 ladyfinger cookies

3 tablespoons sweetened condensed milk

½ teaspoon instant Vietnamese coffee powder, for dusting

MAKE THE COFFEE: Brew the coffee and, while it is still hot, stir in 1 tablespoon of the cocoa and 1½ teaspoons of the cinnamon until they have dissolved. (Reserve the remaining cocoa and cinnamon for assembling.) Set aside and allow the coffee to come to room temperature, then stir in the vanilla extract and set aside.

MAKE THE CREAM: In the bowl of standing mixer fitted with the whisk attachment, beat the egg yolks and sugar at a high speed until very thick, pale, and a ribbon is formed on the surface of the eggs when the whisk is stopped and lifted. Add the mascarpone cheese and beat until medium peaks form, 3 to 4 minutes. Add the heavy cream and a pinch of salt and beat until stiff peaks form, about another 4 minutes. Set aside.

To assemble the tiramisu, have a 7 by 10-inch (17 cm by 25 cm) baking dish ready. Quickly dip a ladyfinger into the coffee mixture, taking care not to oversoak it, then lay it in the dish. Repeat this process until the entire bottom of the baking dish is covered.

Spread half of the cream evenly on top of the ladyfingers, then drizzle the condensed milk over the top. Soak and lay another layer of ladyfingers on top, then spread the rest of the cream on top. Dust the cream with the remaining 1 tablespoon cocoa powder, ½ teaspoon cinnamon, and coffee powder, then wrap with plastic wrap, taking care not to allow the wrap to touch the cream, and refrigerate for at least 3 hours or up to overnight to set before serving. Refrigerate any extra, tightly sealed, for up to 3 days.

Tapioca Pudding with Coconut and Mango

SERVES 2 TO 4 AS A DESSERT

I owe this dish to the women in my life. My wife, Jackie, grew up eating a version of it that is common in Hong Kong dessert shops during trips to see her maternal grandparents, and on a big trip to Asia just before we moved back to Atlanta to open Lazy Betty, she introduced the soupy pudding to me, and I fell in love with the texture. Meanwhile, mangos were one of my mother's favorite fruits, and though I was allergic to them as a kid, I've kicked the allergy and now can fully embrace them as much as I like—and I'm not sure there's a much better dessert combination than coconut and mangos!

Salt

⅓ cup (50 g) dried small tapioca pearls

2 large ripe mangos, peeled and diced (you can substitute peaches or papayas)

⅓ cup (75 ml) bourbon

1 can (13½ ounces / 405 ml) unsweetened full-fat coconut milk

2 tablespoons sorghum syrup

1 pandan leaf (see Note, page 256)

1 teaspoon vanilla extract

In a large saucepan, bring 8 cups (2 L) water and a generous pinch of salt to a boil over high heat. While stirring, pour the tapioca pearls into the water and continue to gently stir so the pearls don't fall to the bottom of the pot and burn. Reduce the heat to medium and cook until almost all the tapioca is translucent, 10 to 15 minutes (it's OK if there are a few pieces with a white speck in the middle, as you don't want to run the risk of overcooking all the tapioca just to get these last few pearls to be translucent). Strain the tapioca through a fine-mesh strainer and place it under cold running water until the tapioca is fully cooled, 30 to 45 seconds, then set aside.

In a food processor, puree roughly three-quarters of the diced mangos until they are smooth (save the rest for garnish). Transfer the puree to a bowl, then cover and refrigerate it.

In a small saucepan, reduce the bourbon over medium heat until roughly 2 tablespoons remain. Add the coconut milk, sorghum syrup, pandan leaf, and vanilla extract to the pot and bring to a boil over medium heat. Stir in a pinch of salt, then transfer the mixture to a medium bowl and let cool to room temperature.

When cool, add the mango puree and tapioca pearls and stir to combine, then cover and chill completely, at least 3 hours or up to overnight. When ready to serve, spoon the pudding into the desired number of dessert glasses or bowls and garnish with the reserved mango.

Rice Pudding with Peaches

SERVES 2 TO 4 AS A DESSERT

Rice is prevalent in many desserts the world over, from steamed mango sticky rice in Thailand to Mexico's arroz con leche, but the most common rice dessert in the South is creamy rice pudding. It's a great blank canvas for ripe summer peaches, and in this recipe, you get to learn how to make a classic crème anglaise custard, a base widely utilized for ice cream, tarts, and (with added starch) pastry cream, which can be used for eclairs, pies, cakes, or the Pandan Banana Pudding on page 255. Take care to whisk the eggs while adding the hot milk; this will temper them and prevent the curdling that happens when their temperature increases too quickly. Also, be sure to use short-grain rice. Not only will it hold its shape well, but its chewy texture will burst with the flavor of the custard after they marry in the refrigerator for a couple hours.

- 1 large egg
- ¼ cup (50 g) sugar
- 1 teaspoon vanilla extract
- ⅓ cup (75 ml) bourbon, reduced to roughly 2 tablespoons by simmering on the stove
- 1 teaspoon ground cinnamon, toasted (preferably Vietnamese) (see Note on page 227)
- Salt
- 1 cup (240 ml) whole milk
- ½ cup (105 g) cooked and cooled short-grain rice
- 2 ripe peaches, cut into rough ½-inch (12 mm) cubes
- Extra chopped peaches (optional)
- Mint leaves (optional)

In a medium bowl, whisk the egg, sugar, vanilla, reduced bourbon, cinnamon, and a pinch of salt to thoroughly combine, then set aside.

In a medium saucepan, bring the milk to a boil over high heat. While whisking the egg mixture, pour in roughly one-third of the hot milk and continue whisking until combined, then pour in another one-third of the milk and whisk to combine to temper the eggs. Pour the milk and egg mixture back into the pot with the remaining one-third hot milk, place over low heat, and cook without boiling while stirring with a rubber spatula, making sure to scrape the corners of the pot to prevent burning, until slightly thickened, 5 to 7 minutes.

Place a fine-mesh sieve over a medium bowl and pour the custard through, straining out and discarding any curdled egg. Add the cooked rice and the peaches, stir well, then cover and refrigerate for at least 2 hours or up to overnight. Serve cold with extra chopped peaches and fresh mint if desired and refrigerate any leftovers for up to 1 week.

Acknowledgments

RON HSU

I'd like to thank Hugh Amano for taking the time out of his life to hear my story, see my city, live my life, and for helping me express it in a way I could not do. I'd also like to thank Rinne Allen for bringing so much comfort, warmth, soul, and depth to my food and for including my family in the process. Many thanks to Rica Allannic and David Black of David Black Literary Agency for taking a leap of faith on a first-time author and for guiding me along the way. Much love and appreciation to the chef behind the scenes, Chef Sierra Pickering, recipe tester and chef annotator, for making the process of writing this book so easy and enjoyable. I'd also like to thank Laura Dozier and Diane Shaw of Abrams for their time, attention, and experience in making this the best book possible. A big shout out goes to Angie Mosier for meeting me and pointing me in the right direction on this book journey. I'd also like to thank Marjorie Speers, who not only helped me with this book, blindly supported and mentored me with materializing Lazy Betty, but also was one of my first customers ever. Much love and appreciation to my wife, Jackie, for enabling me to do the book and for her honest feedback along the way.

I'd also like to acknowledge my late mother, Betty Hsu, who not only instilled in me a sense of hospitality, but also resiliency and grace. Throughout many times when I experienced racism or other types of adversity, I hear her words to keep pushing and to do what's right.

HUGH AMANO

I'd like to thank all the cooks that came before us, those who laid down the traditions that we enjoy and build on today. Many thanks to Ron and his family for opening a door to their delicious, incredibly soulful cuisine. To my agent, Rica Allannic, and the David Black Literary Agency for connecting me to exciting new projects that give me back as much as I put in. And the deepest thanks to Alexis Amano, whose partnership enriches me, keeping me connected to the ground while I explore new heights.

Index

Editor: Laura Dozier
Designer: Danielle Youngsmith
Managing Editor: Krista Keplinger
Production Manager: Kathleen Gaffney

Library of Congress Control Number: 2025941926

ISBN: 978-1-4197-7747-9
eISBN: 979-8-88707-443-6

Printed and bound in China
10 9 8 7 6 5 4 3 2 1

Abrams books are available at special discounts when purchased in quantity for premiums and promotions as well as fundraising or educational use. Special editions can also be created to specification. For details, contact specialsales@abramsbooks.com or the address below.

Abrams® is a registered trademark of Harry N. Abrams, Inc.

ABRAMS is represented in the UK and Europe by Abrams & Chronicle Books, 1 West Smithfield, London EC1A 9JU and Média Participations, 57 rue Gaston Tessier, 75166 Paris, France.
abramsandchronicle.co.uk and media-participations.com
info@abramsandchronicle.co.uk